A Linguistic Model
to Analyze New Testament Greek

A Linguistic Model to Analyze New Testament Greek

Six Examples from Mark One

DAVID RHOADS and TROY MARTIN

 CASCADE *Books* • Eugene, Oregon

A LINGUISTIC MODEL TO ANALYZE NEW TESTAMENT GREEK
Six Examples from Mark One

Copyright © 2025 David Rhoads and Troy Martin. All rights reserved. Except for brief quotations in critical publications or reviews, no part of this book may be reproduced in any manner without prior written permission from the publisher. Write: Permissions, Wipf and Stock Publishers, 199 W. 8th Ave., Suite 3, Eugene, OR 97401.

Cascade Books
An Imprint of Wipf and Stock Publishers
199 W. 8th Ave., Suite 3
Eugene, OR 97401

www.wipfandstock.com

PAPERBACK ISBN: 978-1-60608-165-5
HARDCOVER ISBN: 978-1-4982-8786-9
EBOOK ISBN: 978-4982-4107-6

Cataloging-in-Publication data:

Names: Rhoads, David M., author. | Martin, Troy W., author.

Title: A linguistic model to analyze New Testament Greek : six examples from Mark one / David Rhoads and Troy Martin.

Description: Eugene, OR: Cascade Books, 2025. | Includes bibliographical references.

Identifiers: ISBN: 978-1-60608-165-5 (paperback). | ISBN: 978-1-4982-8786-9 (hardcover). | ISBN: 978-4982-4107-6 (epub).

Subjects: LCSH: Greek language, Biblical. | Bible—New Testament—Language, style. | Bible—New Testament—Greek—Studying and teaching.

Classification: BS1965.2 R46 2025 (print). | BS1965.2 (epub).

VERSION NUMBER 100825

Contents

Preface: Why This Book? | vii

Introduction: How to Use This Book | 1

1 The Beginning of the Gospel: Mark 1:1–8 | 12

2 The Baptism and The Temptation of Jesus: Mark 1:9–13 | 39

3 The Rule of God and the Call of the Disciples: Mark 1:14–20 | 56

4 Jesus the Exorcist: Mark 1:21–28 | 81

5 Jesus the Healer: Mark 1:29–39 | 110

6 Jesus and the Leper: Mark 1:40–45 | 137

Conclusion: What Next? | 163

Bibliography | 165

Preface
Why This Book?

Troy Martin and I teamed up for this project because of a love of language. I had already been well into this project when Troy and I got together to go over the Greek of 1 Peter. We discovered in each other a delight in the details of Greek grammar and syntax and a desire to grasp all the linguistic possibilities of meaning in a passage. When I showed him this project on the Gospel of Mark, he jumped at the chance for us to do it together.

    This book grew out of a weekly practicum session at the Lutheran School of Theology at Chicago. LSTC required all MDiv students to take two quarters of Greek at the beginning of their seminary career. As a means to enable students to keep practicing their Greek after they had completed the basic courses, we faculty in New Testament took turns by semester holding an optional, hour-long session each week as we went over the Greek lectionary lessons for the coming Sunday. The sessions were attended by seminary students as well as candidates in the doctoral program for biblical studies. The sessions served as an opportunity to strengthen Greek skills, all the while instilling the discipline and habit of regular Greek reading.

    Because there was such a wide range of Greek skills and because the students were not expected to prepare in advance, the instructor presumed nothing. Every basic aspect of the Greek passage was explained in each session. So, over the years, I had developed a rather systematic and comprehensive way of going over the Greek of these lectionary passages: orienting the students to the structure and word fields of the passage, identifying the grammatical form of each word or phrase, explaining the syntactical choices for the use of each element of the sentence, discussing the meanings and nuances of the words in the context of the whole writing in which the passage is found, commenting on peculiarities of the style of the writer,

PREFACE

and sharing some reflections on the thematic development of the passage within the larger work.

Students often expressed the desire to have this kind of regular session after they left seminary or graduate school. So, it occurred to me to expand the information I gave in these sessions, put it in a user-friendly format, and make it available in print for wider use—for teachers and preachers, especially for undergraduate, seminary, and graduate students in classes such as Greek or New Testament exegesis or homiletics. This exercise may also assist teachers of Greek to develop a systematic and comprehensive method for reading and teaching. As much as is feasible, the goal here is to make a select number of Greek passages as transparent and as accessible as possible—what it is, how it fits together, what it means—in order to facilitate an understanding of the passage in Greek and to foster the practice of reading Greek carefully and precisely.

This book follows the basic format that I used in the Greek practicum sessions. Here it focuses on the Greek language of six passages, forming the first chapter of the Gospel of Mark. It does not attempt to give an interpretation of the passage either in its ancient context or in regard to its modern relevance. There is no effort to reconstruct history either of the time referred to by the events narrated or of the time of the writer. Nor does it evaluate textual variants or compare the passage to other New Testament writings. It is not a substitute for linguistic commentaries or for standard commentaries or for monographs and articles on particular matters of interpretation.

Rather, the material presented here seeks to fill an important gap between the plain Greek text as it stands before you and the typical commentary. That is, it seeks to provide a thorough analysis of the Greek text as it might then inform matters of interpretation. Many commentaries interpret the text without explaining the basis for the interpretation in the original language. Some computer programs tag the grammatical identification of words and give their basic meanings. Several grammatical commentaries of the New Testament are more helpful, but they often presume a lot of the reader and do not give a full analysis. Up until now, students have had to fill that gap for themselves, usually in a time-consuming process of looking things up in five or six reference works at once and then without guidance as to what to make of the information. What our students wanted was a resource guide in which the process of language analysis is available in one place. The book presented here seeks to meet that need by providing in

Preface

one location the basic information one would need for a thorough understanding of a handful of Greek passages—as a model to emulate for other passages.

At the same time, the approach taken here seeks also to use the occasion to strengthen the reader's understanding and skill in the Greek language. One could infer from this study that the approach might diminish the capacity to do Greek by making readers more dependent on a resource that analyzes the Greek rather than by encouraging readers to analyze and translate independent of such resources. However, by laying out the format in such a way as to strengthen the reader's Greek, the book might then serve to enable the student to be more independent in their use of Greek—with a greater understanding of grammatical forms, with a broader awareness of syntactical choices, and with a deeper appreciation for the dynamics of semantic meaning. Our hope is that this book will serve that purpose.

Troy and I intend this book to be useful to readers at many different levels of language proficiency. For that reason, students who may not be very proficient in Greek might be overwhelmed at first by the amount of material available here. We suggest that readers find their level of comfort.

(1) The general reader who has some familiarity with Greek can begin with the translations, the insights from the discussion of word fields and structure (at the beginning of each chapter), and comments about word meanings and Markan style.

(2) Students who have a basic working knowledge of Greek can also attend to the details of grammatical identification.

(3) Students who are already knowledgeable about grammatical forms may want to concentrate on learning the dynamics of syntax (given in parenthesis after the grammatical identification, often with further discussion to follow), especially in light of the fact that basic Greek classes usually do not teach syntax in a systematic or thorough way.

(4) Advanced students may want to review all of the aspects of the linguistic analysis and then consult the comments on particular difficulties and choices available for the interpretation of the text.

(5) Because we repeat verses, phrases, and words in Greek, students at any level will benefit from reading the Greek silently or aloud when working through the analysis as means to develop facility in reading Greek, and thereby also in understanding it better.

Introduction
How to Use This Book

The purpose of this book is to provide a template for analyzing New Testament Greek. It does so by analyzing six episodes from chapter one of the Gospel of Mark to illustrate the method. The point is to see these exercises as a model for then analyzing other passages in the New Testament.

To accomplish this goal, the analysis of each passage includes parallel text and translation, attention to the word fields in the passage, awareness of the patterns in the text, and the presentation of a close linguistic prototype to identify the grammar and syntax of every phrase and word. The linguistic analysis offers a step-by-step format to follow in making these analyses. The hope is that you will study these passages and then be able to do other passages with greater precision and understanding, and with greater facility. As you complete the work on a passage, review it. Then go to the top of the analysis to practice the method on the Greek without the aid of our analysis, but with the help of the side-by-side English translation readily at hand.

The following comments and explanations will assist you in understanding the format for the analysis of the individual pericopes:

(1) PARALLEL TEXT AND TRANSLATION

Each analysis of a pericope begins with the full text of the episode in parallel with a translation that reflects the grammar, syntax, and semantic meaning of the words in the passage.

- It is divided by sense units to make for easier reading. The translation is set side by side with the Greek so that the reader can practice translating with help.
- Both text and translation are repeated throughout the analysis of lines and words for easy reference.
- We have underlined words that appear in the passage as a means to highlight word fields.

(2) MARKAN WORD FIELDS

There follows a brief discussion of the Markan word fields evident in this passage.

- We are using the phrase "word field" in a non-technical way to refer to the language peculiar to the subject matter that arises in the narrative of Mark. Hence, the language used to describe activity on a Sabbath and the language about sickness and health represent word fields, as does, for example, the language used to talk about purity and defilement or the words related to demonic possession and exorcism.
- Often one word field is embedded in another. For example, talk about eating and fasting is embedded in the larger word field of the rule of God.
- Word fields may be peculiar to a given passage or, more likely, are identified because they occur as a theme across the Gospel. Use of a concordance will be helpful in learning where else in the Gospel word fields are repeated with variation.

The naming and discussion of word fields help to orient and to name for the reader the patterns of language in a pericope. Words do not occur in isolation. They are part of the subject matter being presented. So, it is important to see words in the context of their fields of meaning. Words are part of a culture. Reading Greek is entering another culture expressed by its language. We are here attempting to identify and to draw upon some simple fields of language from the first century represented by the subject matter raised in Mark's Gospel.

(3) STRUCTURE

Next, there will follow a description of the structure of the pericope itself and a description of the way in which the pericope as a whole fits in larger structural patterns in Mark's Gospel. These patterns follow common story-telling techniques in oral discourse.

- On the left. We have marked brief labels to follow the flow of the passage in terms of what happens next and how it follows from what precedes and prepares for what comes next. For example, Setting, Situation, Reply to the Situation.
- On the right, we have also designated lines and phrases with ABAB or abba to indicate parallel and contrasting expressions. Attention to these will illuminate the passage by showing what compares with what and what contrasts with what.

Note: We ae indebted to the work of David Noble for his structural analyses and patterns of parallelism of Markan episodes, which serve as the basis for our own work here.

(4) LINGUISTIC ANALYSIS

The linguistic analysis proceeds verse by verse, phrase by phrase, and word by word. The choice of word clusters for analysis follows the sense units of the sentence and draws upon insights from the discipline of discourse analysis.

Each entry for a word or brief phrase includes the following elements:

(a) Grammatical Identification

Nouns/Pronouns:

1. Case: Nominative (nom), Genitive (gen), Dative (dat), Accusative (acc), Vocative (voc).
2. Number: Singular (sing), Plural (plur).
3. Gender: Masculine (masc), Feminine (fem), Neuter (neut).

Verbs. Tense: Present (pres), Future (fut), Imperfect (Imp), Aorist (aor), Perfect (perf), Pluperfect (plup)

1. Voice: Active (act), Middle (mid), Passive (pass).
2. Mood: Indicative (ind), Subjunctive (subj), Imperative (impv), Optative (opt).
3. Person: First (1st), Second (2nd), or Third (3rd).
4. Number: Singular (sing), Plural (plur).

Participles (hybrid: verbal adjectives)

1. Like verbs, they have tense and voice.
2. Like nouns, they have case, number, and gender.

Infinitives (Hybrid: verbal nouns)

1. Like verbs, they have tense and voice.
2. Like nouns, they have case.

Adverbs (indeclinable)

Conjunctions (indeclinable)

Prepositions (indeclinable)

Along with a Greek grammar, you may wish to use these identifications as an opportunity to review one aspect or another of Greek grammatical forms.

(b) Syntactical Function

In parentheses, the syntactical usage of the word or phrase is identified. In some cases, the syntactical identification is accompanied by an explanation. Every Greek word has both a grammatical form and a syntactical usage. A grammatical form allows for a certain number of possible syntactical uses. You cannot tell from the grammatical form alone what the syntactical usage of that word in the sentence will be. For example, a noun in the accusative case may be a direct object or the object of a preposition or the subject of an infinitive, among other possibilities. The syntactical usage must be determined from the context by studying the relationship of this word to other words in the sentence. Often, a particular word may have more than one possible syntactical function. These different options are the main source (much more than the grammar) of divergent meanings. Along with a book on Greek syntax, you may want to use these identifications as an occasion to review the syntactical choices possible for one particular grammatical form or another.

(c) Semantic Meanings

Following an equal sign (=) there will be a listing of possible translations that reflect the range of semantic meanings for the word or phrase in question. These are drawn from dictionaries, translations, commentaries, and a consideration of the peculiar Markan usage in light of the occurrence of the word here and elsewhere in Mark. The meaning of words is determined by two elements: (1) the range of dictionary meanings available from the language use in the culture in general and (2) the meaning suggested by its immediate context in the pericope and by its larger context within the writing as a whole. Hence, Markan words such as "faith" or "good news" will be informed by the range of meanings present in the culture (dictionary/cultural meanings) and will also have nuances of meaning and connotations that are distinctive to the passage in question and to the Gospel of Mark as a whole. In some cases, we have given extended discussions of the meaning of particular words in Mark's Gospel. For the most part, we have used a word for word translation from Greek to English in order to simplify the Greek analysis.

You may want to use the identification of meaning here as an opportunity to consult several dictionaries and commentaries in order to gain a fuller understanding of these words in the Markan context.

For occurrences of these words in the literature of antiquity outside the Gospel of Mark, consult the resources identified in the bibliography.

(d) Further Observations

There may be further explanations about the grammar, syntax, or semantics of the word or words under discussion. These comments may include observations about distinctive features of the Markan style or structure or word order as well as references to other relevant passages in Mark.

(e) Acknowledgments

This commentary includes insights and observations from other commentators on Markan language usage. These are cited throughout.

(a) Examples: Grammatical Identification of Specific Words

A complete identification of the grammatical form of the word follows immediately after the word as it appears in the text. The identification is always given in a certain order. Using this same format of identification over and over serves as a means to foster the habit of making complete and precise identifications. *This is critical for using this book as a model for a comprehensive analysis of Greek.* Here are some examples from the analyses that follow.

Noun : case, number, gender, type of word (e. g. noun), lexical form (syntax) = **translation**.

- τὸν ἄγγελον acc. sing. masc. of the noun ὁ ἄγγελος (direct object) = **the angel** or **the messenger** or **the ambassador**.
- τῷ προφήτῃ dat. sing. masc. of the noun ὁ προφήτης (simple apposition to τῷ Ἡσαΐᾳ) = **Isaiah, the prophet**.

Article: case, number, gender, type of word (e.g. demonstrative pronoun) lexical form (syntax) = **translation**.

- ὁ nom. sing. masc. of the definite article ὁ, ἡ, τό (a substantive use of the article, functioning as the subject and serving as a demonstrative pronoun) = **"he (the leper)."**
- ἡ ἀκοή nom. sing. fem. of the noun ἡ ἀκοή (subject). The noun ἀκοή expresses a passive sense of what is heard = **"the report."**

Adjective: case, number, gender, type of word (e. g. adjective), lexical form (syntax) = **translation**.

- διδαχὴ καινή anarthrous nom. sing. fem. of the noun ἡ διδαχή, modified by the nom. sing. fem. of the adjective καινός, -ή, -όν (apposition or predicate nominative) = "**a new teaching**."
- τοῖς πνεύμασι τοῖς ἀκαθάρτοις dat. plur. neut. of the noun τὸ πνεῦμα, modified in the attributive position by the dat. plur. neut of the adjective ἀκάθαρτος, -η, ον (dative as direct object/complement of verbs of commanding).

Pronoun: case, number, gender, type of word (e. g. pronoun), lexical form (syntax) = **translation**.

- μου gen. sing. of the 1st pers. personal pronoun ἐγώ (genitive of possession or genitive of relationship) = **my [messenger]**.
- ὑμᾶς acc. plur. of the 2nd pers. personal pronoun σύ (direct object) = **you** (plural).

Relative pronoun: case, number, gender, type of word (e. g. pronoun), lexical form (syntax) = **translation**.

- οὗ gen. sing. masc. of the relative pronoun ὅ (possessive pronoun) = "**whose [strap]**."

Verb: tense, voice, mood, person, number, type of word (e. g. verb), lexical form (syntax) = **translation**.

- ἀποστέλλω pres. act. ind. 1st pers. sing. of the verb ἀποστέλλω (present of intention, with future force) = **I (intend to) send** or **I am going to send** or **I will send**.
- ποιεῖτε pres. act. impv. 2nd pers. plur. of the verb ποιέω (present command, calling for ongoing action) = **make**.
- ἐκήρυσσεν impf. act. ind. 3rd pers. sing. of the verb κηρύσσω (either an imperfect of repeated action or an imperfect of customary action) = **he was preaching** or **he would proclaim**.
- Φιμώθητι aor. pass. impv. 2nd pers. sing. of the verb φιμόω (aorist imperative commanding a single action) = "**be muzzled**" (literally, like an ox—in its original meaning) or "**shut up**," or "**keep quiet**" or "**Silence!**"

Participles: tense, voice, type of word (e. g. participle), case, number, gender, lexical form (syntax) = **translation**.

- παρακαλῶν pres. act. participle nom. sing. masc. of the verb παρακαλέω, agreeing with the subject (λεπρός) of the main clause (a circumstantial participle that, as a present, depicts action contemporaneous with the time of the main verb/ depicts the "manner" by which the leper comes to him) = "**begging**" or "**beseeching**" or "**pleading with**" or "**imploring**."
- παράγων pres. act. participle nom. sing. masc. of the verb παράγω, agreeing with the subject of the main verb εἶδεν (a circumstantial participle of time which, in the present tense, expresses action contemporaneous with the time of the main verb) = "**passing along**" or "**while going along**."

Infinitives: : tense, voice, type of word (e. g. infinitive), lexical form (syntax) = **translation**.

- ἀπολέσαι aor. act. inf. of the verb ἀπόλλυμι (a complementary infinitive after ἔρχομαι, expressing purpose) = "**to destroy**" or "**in order to destroy**."
- εἰσελθεῖν 2nd aor. act. inf. of the deponent verb ἔρχομαι, (complementary infinitive after the auxilliary/modal verb δύνασθαι, which is also in the form of an infinitive in the aorist, expressing an action occurring without respect to time = "**to enter**."
- κηρύσσειν pres, act. infinitive of the verb κηρύσσω (complementary infinitive to the auxiliary verb ἄρχομαι, the present tense of the infinitive expressing ongoing action) = "**to proclaim**."

Adverb: indeclinable. Type of word (e. g. adverb) = lexical form (syntax) = **translation**.

- εὐθύς adverb (modifying the finite verb and not the participle, telling *when* Jesus drove him out) = **immediately**.
- εὐθύς adverb (temporal) = "**at once**" or "**immediately**." Εὐθύς here emphasizes the rapidity with which the word about Jesus spread as a consequence of Jesus' exorcism of the unclean spirit.

Introduction

Prepositional phrases: explanation of preposition and object of the preposition, lexical form (syntax) = **translation**.

- εἰς τὴν Γαλιλαίαν prepositional phrase (expressing motion toward and into) with εἰς + the accusative, here the acc. sing. fem of the noun ἡ Γαλιλαία = "**into Galilee.**"
- ἐν τῇ θαλάσσῃ prepositional phrase (expressing place where) with ἐν + the dative, here the dat. sing. fem. of the noun ἡ θάλασσα (dative of place where) = "**in the sea.**"
- ἐν τῷ 'Ησαΐᾳ prep. phrase with ἐν + the dative, here the dat. sing. masc. of the proper name ὁ 'Ησαΐα (object of the preposition/ dative of place where) = **in Isaiah.**
- ἐν πνεύματι ἁγίῳ prepositional phrase (expressing means) with ἐν + the dative, here dat. sing. neut. of the noun τὸ πνεῦμα modified by dat. sing. neut. of the adjective ἅγιος (object of the preposition/ dative of means) = **with [the] holy spirit** or **in the Holy Spirit**.

Conjunction: Type of word (e. g. conjunction=lexical form) (syntax) = **translation.**

- Καθώς conj. (comparative with causal semantics) = **according as** or **just as** or **because.**
- καί coord. conj. (simple connective for the two participles) = **and.**
- δέ postpositive coor. conj. (adversative) = **but** or **by contrast.**
- καί coord. conj. (paratactic, connecting this sentence to the previous one) = "**and.**"
- ὥστε subord. conj. (introduces a result clause + an infinitive) = "**so that**" or "**with the result [that].**"
- γάρ postpositive subord. conj. (explanatory) = "**for.**" This clause explains why they were amazed.

Interjections: (indeclinable) Grammatical identification (syntax) = **translation.**

- 'Ιδού demonstrative particle (interjection that serves to call attention to and emphasize what follows) = **look!** or **behold!**

(5) **Preview**. At the end of each pericope, a preview paragraph offers a transition by looking ahead to the material that follows this passage in the Markan narrative, with some comments on the relevance of subsequent episodes to the pericope under study.

Conclusion. Reading the commentary on a particular passage from beginning to end may be the first step in understanding and interpreting the passage. Then, you may want to consult other commentaries on the passage. Perhaps, you will come back to particular verses or words to clarify some point as you further develop your thinking on the passage. Or you may simply want to use this book as a guide for practicing and learning Greek in general. In any case, we hope that you will benefit from these linguistic comments in ways that will enhance your study of New Testament Greek.

TIPS TO BENEFIT FROM THIS BOOK

1. Read the Greek as you go, either silently or, better, aloud. This will make your reading easier and improve your understanding. We have deliberately repeated the Greek often, so that you can follow the points being made and still stay close to the Greek.

2. Always remember that we are analyzing the story world of Mark's narrative. No comments relate to the historicity of the text. Just as a film or a novel creates a world in its own right, so does Mark, understood as a story.

3. The idea is to learn how to parse words and lines in a certain order that involves a complete analysis. Even if you are very familiar with the analysis of a particular word, repeat it nonetheless. It will make everything easier once you have learned the patterns of analysis.

4. Mark has a deceptively spare style, saying and implying much in few words. The vocabulary is limited. There are no flourishes in Mark. He uses everyday language that lends itself to oral narration. Do not be fooled by this. The plot lines are complex and the literary/oral patterns of storytelling are complex. And it is tight. Attention to this will help you to understand Mark's Greek better.

5. We have sought to foster a word for word translation close to the Greek. We have avoided paraphrasing and generalizing. We have tried to

Introduction

keep the word order where it makes sense in English, but note Mark's word order and its rhetorical impact.

6. We repeat the patterns of analysis with every word. This is designed to assist you in learning a method to interpret.

1

The Beginning of the Gospel
Mark 1:1–8

PREVIEW

This passage is the opening of the Gospel of Mark. The author begins with an announcement of the subject matter of his whole story and immediately cites the words of God from Isaiah as the driving force behind the events and personages to be depicted in this passage. The narrator wastes no time in showing the fulfillment of Isaiah's prophecy in the person and activity of John the Baptist. In turn, John prophesies the impending appearance of one greater than he is. In these few verses, we readers are prepared to welcome Jesus on the scene as "the anointed one, the son of God."

‹1:1› Ἀρχὴ τοῦ <u>εὐαγγελίου Ἰησοῦ Χριστοῦ</u> [<u>υἱοῦ θεοῦ</u>].

‹1:2› Καθὼς <u>γέγραπται</u> ἐν τῷ Ἠσαΐᾳ <u>τῷ προφήτῃ</u>,
   Ἰδοὺ <u>ἀποστέλλω</u> τὸν <u>ἄγγελόν</u> μου
     πρὸ προσώπου σου,
   ὃς <u>κατασκευάσει</u> <u>τὴν ὁδόν</u> σου·
  ‹1:3› φωνὴ βοῶντος <u>ἐν τῇ ἐρήμῳ</u>,
   Ἑτοιμάσατε <u>τὴν ὁδὸν</u> κυρίου,

The beginning of the <u>good news</u> about <u>Jesus</u> [the] <u>anointed one</u>, [<u>son of God</u>].

Just as it <u>is written</u> in Isaiah <u>the prophet</u>,
   "Look! I <u>am sending</u> my <u>messenger</u>
     before your presence,
   who <u>will prepare</u> your <u>way</u>,
  the voice of one shouting <u>in the desert</u>,
   'Make ready the <u>way</u> of the Lord,

εὐθείας ποιεῖτε τὰς τρίβους αὐτοῦ,	Make straight his paths'"—
‹1:4› ἐγένετο <u>Ἰωάννης</u> [ὁ] <u>βαπτίζων ἐν τῇ ἐρήμῳ</u>	<u>John</u> appeared <u>baptizing</u> <u>in the desert</u>
καὶ <u>κηρύσσων βάπτισμα</u> μετανοίας	and <u>proclaiming</u> a <u>baptism</u> of repentance
εἰς ἄφεσιν <u>ἁμαρτιῶν</u>.	for the pardon of <u>sins</u>.
‹1:5› καὶ ἐξεπορεύετο πρὸς αὐτὸν <u>πᾶσα</u> ἡ Ἰουδαία χώρα	And going out to him were <u>all</u> the Judean countryside
καὶ οἱ Ἱεροσολυμῖται <u>πάντες</u>,	and <u>all</u> the Jerusalemites,
καὶ <u>ἐβαπτίζοντο ὑπ' αὐτοῦ ἐν τῷ Ἰορδάνῃ ποταμῷ</u>	and they <u>were being baptized</u> <u>by him</u> <u>in the river Jordan</u>
ἐξομολογούμενοι <u>τὰς ἁμαρτίας</u> αὐτῶν.	while acknowledging publicly their <u>sins</u>.
‹1:6› καὶ ἦν ὁ <u>Ἰωάννης</u> ἐνδεδυμένος τρίχας καμήλου	Now <u>John</u> was dressed in camel's hair
καὶ ζώνην δερματίνην περὶ τὴν ὀσφὺν αὐτοῦ,	with a leather belt around his waist
καὶ ἐσθίων ἀκρίδας καὶ μέλι ἄγριον.	and was eating locusts and wild honey.
‹1:7› καὶ <u>ἐκήρυσσεν</u> λέγων,	And he <u>was proclaiming</u> (saying),
"Ἔρχεται ὁ ἰσχυρότερός μου ὀπίσω μου,	"After me comes the one stronger than I am;
οὗ οὐκ εἰμὶ ἱκανὸς κύψας	I am not worthy after stooping (down)
λῦσαι τὸν ἱμάντα τῶν ὑποδημάτων αὐτοῦ.	to untie the straps of his sandals.
‹1:8› <u>ἐγὼ ἐβάπτισα</u> ὑμᾶς ὕδατι,	<u>I baptized</u> you with water,
<u>αὐτὸς</u> δὲ <u>βαπτίσει</u> ὑμᾶς ἐν πνεύματι ἁγίῳ.	but <u>he</u> <u>will baptize</u> you with holy spirit."

MARKAN WORD FIELDS

There are four word fields here. The overall word field is (1) the "announcement of a coming ruler." Within this word field is embedded the dynamic of (2) "prophecy and fulfillment." Within the word field of prophecy and fulfillment occur two other word fields: (3) "the way" and (4) "baptism."

"The Announcement of a Coming Ruler"

Almost everything in this passage relates to the arrival of a new ruler. The word "gospel" (τοῦ εὐαγγελίου) was used in the culture to announce the inauguration of a new ruler and to proclaim the arrival of that ruler to be received by the people. The epithets of "messiah" or "anointed one" (Χριστοῦ) and "son of God" (υἱοῦ θεοῦ) are both royal designations. The declaration of what "has been written" (γέγραπται) and the account of its fulfillment give solemnity and divine authorization to the announcement. The description of a "voice shouting in the desert" (φωνὴ βοῶντος ἐν τῇ ἐρήμῳ,) and the call to "Prepare the way of the lord" (Ἑτοιμάσατε τὴν ὁδὸν κυρίου) characterize a royal proclamation. Then John's call for "repentance" (μετανοίας) and his announcement that "one stronger than I am comes after me" (Ἔρχεται ὁ ἰσχυρότερός μου ὀπίσω μου) emphasize the importance of the figure who is about to appear. John is "not worthy to untie the straps of his sandals" (οὐκ εἰμὶ ἱκανὸς κύψας λῦσαι τὸν ἱμάντα τῶν ὑποδημάτων αὐτου) and, unlike John, the coming one "will baptize you in holy spirit" (βαπτίσει ὑμᾶς ἐν πνεύματι ἁγίῳ). The form and content of the language in this whole passage conveys an ethos of expectation, anticipation, and preparation for a ruler who is about to appear.

"Prophecy and Fulfillment"

Embedded within this announcement of a new ruler, is a word field that quotes a prophecy and then describes its fulfillment. The words "in Isaiah the prophet" (ἐν τῷ Ἡσαΐᾳ τῷ προφήτῃ) form the first thrust of prophecy here. The author states that the beginning of the good news happened according to these words.

This prophecy calls for people to prepare for the arrival of a new ruler. In Isaiah's context, this preparation was depicted as the straightening and smoothing of the road through the desert from Babylon toward Jerusalem for a new era of freedom from exile and oppression. In Mark, this prophecy is used metaphorically of the preparation for the coming of "Jesus the anointed one, the son of God" (Ἰησοῦ Χριστοῦ [υἱοῦ θεοῦ), who is the agent to usher in God's rulership over Israel and the world. God is sending John as an ambassador/messenger ahead of Jesus to announce his coming and to prepare the people for it.

This passage from the prophecy of Isaiah 40:3 (and Malachi 3:1) is then explained by treating it as an allegory for John the baptizer, his message, and his work. He is the "messenger" (τὸν ἄγγελόν) "crying out" (βοῶντος) "in the desert" (ἐν τῇ ἐρήμῳ) announcing "the one coming after him" (Ἔρχεται ὁ ἰσχυρότερός μου ὀπίσω μου) and urging the people to prepare by participating in a "baptism of repentance" (βάπτισμα μετανοίας) leading to "the pardoning of sins" (εἰς ἄφεσιν ἁμαρτιῶν). People respond by "coming out to him" (ἐξεπορεύετο πρὸς αὐτὸν), "confessing their sins," (ἐξομολογούμενοι τὰς ἁμαρτίας αὐτῶν), "being baptized" (ἐβαπτίζοντο ὑπ' αὐτου), and having their sins pardoned. Each of these details corresponds, as (allegorical) fulfillment, to some aspect of the prophecy the narrator quotes.

The word field of prophecy and fulfillment continues, because John not only fulfills prophecy but in turn prophesies of the one coming after him, who is much greater than John—whose sandals John is "not worthy even to stoop down and unstrap" (οὗ οὐκ εἰμὶ ἱκανὸς κύψας λῦσαι τὸν ἱμάντα) and who will baptize with holy spirit (βαπτίσει ὑμᾶς ἐν πνεύματι ἁγίω). This prophetic role of John is reinforced by the clothing he wears and the food he eats. Being "dressed in camel's hair with a leather belt around his waist" (ἐνδεδυμένος τρίχας καμήλου καὶ ζώνην δερματίνην περὶ τὴν ὀσφὺν αὐτοῦ) and "eating locusts and wild honey" (ἐσθίων ἀκρίδας καὶ μέλι ἄγριον) recalls the figure of Elijah, who was expected to return at the end time (2 Kings 1:8 and Malachi 4:5-6). The equating of John as the latter-day Elijah figure is later confirmed in the words of the Markan Jesus, who says that "Elijah has already come" (9:11-13). The pericope ends without the stated fulfillment of John's prophecy, but the reader by now has no doubt that the story will soon narrate the fulfillment.

Hence, there is a succession of prophecy and fulfillment—Isaiah to John to Jesus to others. Prophecies are driving forces in the narrative, for oracles that come from God not only presage events but also help to generate them. Prophecy and fulfillment provide many of the verbal threads that weave this narrative together through foreshadowing and retrospection, anticipation and echo, cause and effect.

"The Way"

Embedded within the word field of prophecy and fulfillment is the motif of "the way." The prophecy announces that people are to "Prepare the way of the Lord; make his paths level" (Ἑτοιμάσατε τὴν ὁδὸν κυρίου, εὐθείας ποιεῖτε τὰς τρίβους αὐτοῦ) The story expresses this "way" with the movement of people across landscape. John is baptizing "in the river Jordan" (ἐν τῷ Ἰορδάνῃ ποταμῷ) "in the desert" (ἐν τῇ ἐρήμῳ). The people come out from the whole countryside of Judea (πᾶσα ἡ Ἰουδαία χώρα) and from Jerusalem (οἱ Ἱεροσολυμῖται πάντες) to be baptized by him. Soon Jesus will come from Galilee to be baptized, and, after John is arrested, Jesus will appear in Galilee to begin his ministry. Jesus' subsequent movement throughout Galilee eventually leads to Jerusalem and to execution.

Through the whole narrative of the Gospel, the author uses the word "way" (ἡ ὁδός) as a recurring verbal thread that keeps the motif of the journey before the reader. In this way, the geographical movement in the story becomes a metaphorical manifestation for the behavior and outcome of living "the way of God." John proclaims, is handed over, and is put to death. Jesus proclaims, is handed over, and is put to death. The disciples proclaim, will be handed over, and will be put to death. The word field of "the way" (initially used here to depict entrance and then journey) becomes a metaphor to depict the commitments and consequences of those who will live faithfully in response to the rule of God.

"Baptism"

Also embedded in the word field of prophecy and fulfillment is the word field of baptism. John comes baptizing in the desert. He proclaims a "baptism of repentance" for "the pardoning of sins." People respond by "coming out" to the desert, "confessing their sins," "being baptized," and having their sins pardoned. As we shall see, this baptism is *not* presented as a rite of entrance to be repeated in the ongoing life of the community of Jesus' followers. Rather, in Mark, the baptism is the work of John leading to repentance by the people in preparation for the one coming. When the stronger one arrives, John's baptism of water will no longer be needed, for Jesus will baptize/touch people with the holy spirit—through his work of exorcism, healing, and teaching.

"The Rule of God"

It is not yet apparent at this point in the narrative, but the overarching word field for Mark's story is "establishing of the rule of God" over the cosmos. In this episode, the word "gospel" and related language anticipates the arrival of the rule of God. To announce the coming of the stronger one is to announce the coming of God's rule. This is confirmed by the shift that will soon take place: John has announced the coming of Jesus, and Jesus in turn will announce the arrival of the rule of God.

STRUCTURE

This passage is part of the prologue (1:1–15), designed to introduce key words, motifs, and characters and to set the stage for the whole story. It is the "beginning" of the good news about Jesus. This pericope has four parts: the title (1:1); the prophecy from scripture (1:2–3); the description of the fulfillment of the prophecy in the appearance and activity of John (1:4–5); and the prophecies of John about the one coming after him (1:6–8) (Noble 401).

Setting

   Setting.
   <1:1> The beginning of the good news about Jesus [the] anointed one, [son of God].
   <1:2> Just as it is written in Isaiah the prophet,

   Situation
      "Look! I am sending my messenger before your presence, a
         who will prepare your way   b

   Reply to the situation
   <1:3> the voice of one shouting in the desert,   a
      'Prepare the way of the Lord,   b
      Make straight his paths.'"—

Situation

   Setting
   <1:4> John appeared baptizing in the desert   a
      and proclaiming a baptism of repentance for the pardon of sins. b

   Situation
   <1:5> And going out to him were all the Judean countryside
      and all the Jerusalemites,

   Reply to the situation
   and they were being baptized by him in the Jordan River   a
      acknowledging publicly their sins.

Reply to the situation

   Situation
   <1:6> Now John was dressed in camel's hair
      with a leather belt around his waist

and was eating locusts and wild honey.

Reply to the situation
<1:7> And he was proclaiming (saying), b
"After me comes the one stronger than I am; a
I am not worthy after stooping (down) b
to untie the straps of his sandals.
<1:8> I baptized you with water, b
but he will baptize you with holy spirit" a

You can see from the ab ab parallels how patterns are replicated in each of the sections. The parallels help to interpret each other. That is, the second ab pattern of a section elaborates and gives more information about the first ab pattern in that section, in each case clarifying the nature of John's role and his message. The ab ba pattern at the end explains the relationship between John and Jesus: the first a and the final a show that what makes the coming one stronger than John is that he will baptize in holy spirit. The first b and the second b show that what makes John inferior to the coming one is that he only baptizes in water.

LINGUISTIC COMMENTARY

<1:1> Ἀρχὴ τοῦ εὐαγγελίου Ἰησοῦ Χριστοῦ [υἱοῦ θεοῦ]. = **The beginning of the good news about Jesus [the] anointed one, [the] son of God**

Ἀρχὴ τοῦ εὐαγγελίου Ἰησοῦ Χριστοῦ [υἱοῦ θεοῦ].

- Ἀρχή nom. sing. fem. of the noun ἡ ἀρχή.' (hanging nominative or subject) = "**The beginning**" or "**The start**." Ἀρχή is without the article, but translated as if it had an article because it is yoked with a genitive that does have an article (cf. Williams 18). There are three options for the syntax here: (1) the whole phrase is a hanging nominative (or a nominative independent—Smyth 940-41; Wallace 49-50; Decker 1), which stands alone as a title or as a subject to be picked up in the following sentence = "**The beginning . . . . Just as it is written in;**" (2) The subject of a sentence whose verb ἦν ("was") has been elided = "**the beginning . . . [was] just as it has been written;**" or (3) The subject of a sentence whose verb is ἐγένετο (in vs. 4), whereby the intervening quotation is treated as an interjection = "**the beginning . . .[—just**

as it has been written. . . make straight the his paths]—was John baptizing in the desert."

The "beginning" of the good news may refer to the whole story of Mark (which begins the history of proclaiming the good news up to Mark's time, Decker 1) or the "beginning" may simply refer to the first part of Mark's story, namely, the part about John and the baptism of Jesus (Williams 12). All of this is part of the prologue of Mark's Gospel (1:1–15) that introduces themes, key words, characters, and events to the reader and foreshadows much that will happen later.

- τοῦ εὐαγγελίου gen. sing. neut. of the noun τὸ εὐαγγέλιον (partitive genitive, the "good news" being the whole of which the "beginning" is a part) = "**[the beginning] of the good news.**"
- Ἰησοῦ Χριστοῦ gen. sing. masc, of the formal name ὁ Ἰησοῦς combined with the gen. sing. masc. of the adjective χριστός, -ή, όν = "**Jesus, the one who has been anointed.**" The adjective χριστός is a verbal adjective with the suffix -τος and has the meaning of a perfect passive participle (Smyth 471–72). It is formed from the aorist passive stem of the verb χρίω = "**the one who has been anointed.**"

Χριστοῦ functions either as the second part of Jesus' name = "**Jesus Christ**" or "**Jesus Anointed**" or "**Jesus Messiah**" or as an epithet in apposition to Ἰησοῦ, translated either as "**Jesus, the anointed one**" or as "**Jesus, anointed one.**" The syntax of these two as genitives in relation to the head noun τοῦ εὐαγγελίου is either (1) a subjective genitive, in which case, the good news is the news that Jesus (as the subject of the action implied in the verbal noun "good news") proclaims (= "**the good news of [proclaimed by] Jesus**") or (2) an objective genitive, in which case Jesus is the object of the action of proclaiming implied in the verbal noun of "good news" (= "**the good news of [about] Jesus**" (Decker 2). Because the whole story is about Jesus and not just his proclamation, we prefer the latter interpretation.

- [υἱοῦ gen. sing. masc. of the noun ὁ υἱός (genitive of apposition, either as a second noun in apposition to Ἰησοῦ (= "**Jesus, the anointed one, the son of God**") or in apposition to the whole phrase Ἰησοῦ Χριστοῦ ("**Jesus Christ, son of God**") (Decker 2).
- [θεοῦ] gen. sing. masc. of the noun θεός (genitive of relationship) = "**[the son] of God.**" If one treats the two genitives χριστοῦ and υἱοῦ as separate and sequential appositions to Ἰησοῦ, there is a typical Markan

two step progression in which the first step ("the anointed one") gives a general identification of Jesus, while the second step ("the son of God") gives a more specific and more telling identification of Jesus. The two parts correspond to the two parts of the Gospel as a whole, in which the first part climaxes in Peter's confession of Jesus as "the anointed one" (8:29) and the second part climaxes in the centurion's confession of Jesus as "the son of God" (15:39).

<1:2> Καθὼς γέγραπται ἐν τῷ Ἠσαΐᾳ τῷ προφήτῃ, Ἰδοὺ ἀποστέλλω τὸν ἄγγελόν μου πρὸ προσώπου σου, ὃς κατασκευάσει τὴν ὁδόν σου· = **Just as it stands written in Isaiah the prophet, "Look! I am sending my messenger before your presence, who will prepare your way.**

Καθὼς γέγραπται ἐν τῷ Ἠσαΐᾳ τῷ προφήτῃ,

- Καθώς conj. (comparative, with causal semantics; see BDAG καθώς 3.) = "**according as**" or "**just as**" or "**because**." Καθώς is a combination of κατά (according to) and ὡς (as). The word implies a comparison between what was prophesied and the events about to be described. It may also imply a causal relationship, that is, that the events are happening as a result of the prophesy.

- γέγραπται perf. pass. ind. 3rd pers. sing. of the verb γράφω (the perfect tense emphasizing a past event whose force continues into the present) = "**it has been written**" or "**it is written**" or "**it stands written**" (Williams 20). This verb along with the conjunction καθώς forms a citation formula introducing a scriptural quotation (Decker 3).

- ἐν τῷ Ἠσαΐᾳ prep. phrase with ἐν + the dative, here the dat. sing. masc. of the proper name ὁ Ἠσαΐα (object of the preposition/ dative of place where) = "**in Isaiah**." Because the reference is to the scroll or writing of Isaiah (note the "it stands written"), ἐν can be translated "in the book of" and takes a dative of place where (Decker 3).

- τῷ προφήτῃ dat. sing. masc. of the noun ὁ προφήτης (simple apposition to τῷ Ἠσαΐᾳ) = "**Isaiah, the prophet**."

Ἰδοὺ ἀποστέλλω τὸν ἄγγελόν μου πρὸ προσώπου σου,

- Ἰδού demonstrative particle (serves to call attention to and emphasize what follows) = "**look!**" or "**behold!**" When the letters ιδου have an acute accent, the word is to be identified as a demonstrative particle (BDAG ἰδού). If, however, the manuscript letters ιδου were to be accented with a circumflex (ἰδοῦ), the word would be a 2nd aor. mid. imperative 2nd person sing. of the verb ὁράω = "**look**" (Decker 3–4).

- ἀποστέλλω pres. act. ind. 1st pers. sing. of the verb ἀποστέλλω (present of intention, with future force) = "**I (intend to) send**" or "**I am (going to be) sending**" or "**I will send**."

- τὸν ἄγγελον acc. sing. masc. of the noun ὁ ἄγγελος (direct object) = "**the angel**" or "**the messenger**."

- μου gen. sing. of the 1st pers. personal pronoun ἐγώ (genitive of possession or genitive of relationship) = "**my [messenger]**."

- πρὸ προσώπου prepositional phrase with πρό + the genitive, here the gen. sing. neut. of the noun τὸ προσώπον (object of the preposition) = "**before [your] face**" or "**ahead of your presence**" (Decker 4).

- σου gen. sing. of the 2nd pers. personal pronoun (possessive genitive or partitive genitive) = "**your face**." Because the word "face" is a metonym (a part [face] that stands for the whole [Lord]), the phrase can mean = "**before your presence**" or simply "**before you**."

- ὅς nom. sing. masc. of the relative pronoun ὅς agreeing in number and gender with its antecedent (τὸν ἄγγελον) while its case (nominative) is determined by its function in the relative clause (subject) = "**who**."

- κατασκευάσει fut. act. ind. 3rd sing. of the verb κατασκευάζω (punctiliar future referring to the preparation as a single act or as a global future referring to all the acts of preparation as one) = "**will prepare**."

- τὴν ὁδόν acc. sing. fem. of the noun ἡ ὁδός, a second declension feminine noun (direct object) = "**the way**" or "**the road**" or "**the path**." The word ὁδός is a significant verbal thread in Mark, signifying the motif of the way of God. Often this word is translated differently in various contexts: path, way, journey, road, and so on. Attention to the recurrence of the Greek word ὁδός will clarify how significant it is for the Markan portrayal of characters: John (who prepares the way), Jesus (who leads the way) and his disciples (who follow the way).

- σου gen. sing. of the 2nd pers. personal pronoun σύ (genitive of possession, identifying whose path is being prepared) = "**your**." The antecedent of the pronoun is "the Lord."

<1:3> φωνὴ βοῶντος ἐν τῇ ἐρήμῳ, Ἑτοιμάσατε τὴν ὁδὸν κυρίου, εὐθείας ποιεῖτε τὰς τρίβους αὐτοῦ, = **the voice of one shouting in the desert, 'Make ready the way of the Lord, Make straight his paths.'"—**

φωνὴ βοῶντος ἐν τῇ ἐρήμῳ,

- φωνὴ anarthrous nom. sing, fem. of the noun ἡ φωνή (which, when combined with a genitive, may be treated as a definite noun) = **"voice"** or **"the voice."** In terms of the syntax of φωνή as a nominative, this word and the whole verse that goes with it is an appositive. To be in apposition, φωνή must be in the same case as the noun or pronoun to which it serves as an apposition. φωνή is in apposition to ὅς. Of course, the antecedent of ὅς is ἄγγελον. So φωνή does specify ἄγγελον, but it links approximately to ὅς and not to ἄγγελον.

- βοῶντος pres. act. participle gen. sing. masc. of the verb βοάω (a substantive use of the participle) = **"of one shouting."** The genitive is partitive, the genitive being the whole (person) of which the voice is a part.

- ἐν τῇ ἐρήμῳ prepositional phrase with ἐν + the dative, here the dat. sing. fem. of the adjective ἔρημος (a substantive use of the adjective with a feminine article/ object of the preposition/ dative of place where) = **"in the desert."** This prepositional phrase may go with one of two words. (1) It may modify βοῶντος, thereby identifying where John was shouting = **"shouting in the desert, 'Prepare the way.'"** Or (2) it may go with the verb Ἑτοιμάσατε, calling for the preparation to take place in the wilderness = **"shouting, 'In the desert, prepare the way.'"** Supporting the latter reading is the fact that, in the narrative, all the people and Jesus go into the desert of Judea. In this interpretation, the preparation actually begins in the perilous and dangerous wilderness of the desert. If this latter interpretation is preferred, the punctuation of the sentence in translation (capitalization, commas, and quotation marks) will change.

Ἑτοιμάσατε τὴν ὁδὸν κυρίου,

- Ἑτοιμάσατε aor. act. impv. 2nd pers. plur. of the verb ἑτοιμάζω (specific command) = **"prepare"** or **"make ready."** The aorist imperative commands the action globally as a whole rather than as ongoing action (Wallace 485). Hence, the command is not to prepare generally, but to prepare specifically on a particular occasion and in a particular location. This conforms with the idea that the repentance John calls for is not the ongoing repentance in the life of a follower; rather, the repentance called for here is specifically and only the preparation that precedes the appearance of Jesus.

- τὴν ὁδόν acc. sing. fem. of the second declension noun ἡ ὁδός (direct object of the imperative) = "**the way.**"
- κυρίου gen. sing. masc. of the noun ὁ κύριος (genitive of possession, identifying whose way is being prepared) = "**of the Lord.**" The anarthrous form does not make this word indefinite. The term *Lord* may refer to Jesus or God. Since Mark is reticent to reference Jesus as Lord except with the meaning owner or sir (Mark 2:28; 7:28; cf. 11:3), the ambiguous reference is more likely to God, although a reference to Jesus may also be intended (Decker 4–5).

εὐθείας ποιεῖτε τὰς τρίβους αὐτοῦ,

- εὐθείας acc. plur. fem. of the adjective εὐθύς (adjectival accusative after a verb that takes a double accusative) = "**straight**" (Decker 5).
- ποιεῖτε pres. act. impv. 2nd pers. plur. of the verb ποιέω (present command, calling for ongoing action) = "**make.**" The imperative is in the present tense because the action is indefinite. The action is indefinite because "making straight paths" is only part of the definite action of preparing. The aorist imperative (Ἑτοιμάσατε) states the total action, while the present imperative (ποιεῖτε) states a part of the total action (cf. 1 Peter 2:17).
- τὰς τρίβους acc. plur. fem. of the second declension noun ἡ τρίβος (direct object of the imperative) = "**the paths**" or "**the roads.**"
- αὐτοῦ gen. sing. masc. of the 3rd pers. personal pronoun αὐτός (genitive of possession, identifying whose "paths" are "made straight") = "**[the paths] of him**" or "**his [roads]**." The antecedent of the pronoun αὐτοῦ is κυρίου.

<1:4> ἐγένετο Ἰωάννης [ὁ] βαπτίζων ἐν τῇ ἐρήμῳ καὶ κηρύσσων βάπτισμα μετανοίας εἰς ἄφεσιν ἁμαρτιῶν. = **John appeared baptizing in the desert and proclaiming a baptism of repentance for pardon of sins.**

ἐγένετο Ἰωάννης [ὁ] βαπτίζων ἐν τῇ ἐρήμῳ

- ἐγένετο aor. mid. (in form) ind. 3rd pers. sing. of the deponent verb γίνομαι (equative verb or equative verb in a periphrastic construction or an intransitive verb) = "**was**" or "**was baptizing**" or "**appeared baptizing**." The grammatical designation "deponent" categorizes verbs that are active in meaning but middle or passive in form (Wallace 428–30). The term comes from the Latin verb *deponere*, which means to lay aside. Thus, a deponent verb lays aside its middle or passive form to express an active meaning. Although frequently explained in most biblical Greek grammars, the category of the deponent verb has recently received much criticism (Pennington 55–76, 181–203; Taylor 167–76). The essential criticism is that the "active in meaning" refers to the voice of the verb in the English Language, not the Greek. Critics argue that the middle or passive form of so-called deponent verbs retain the essential meaning of the middle voice by which the action performed by the subject of the verb somehow affects, involves, or comes back upon the subject. In the case of the verb γίνομαι, the being, happening, or existing expressed by this verb necessarily affects the subject of the verb.

The verb ἐγένετο may mark the beginning of a sentence or it may be connected to the material that precedes it. There are three options here. (1) Ἀρχή may be the subject of ἐγένετο, in which case the intervening prophecy would be an interjection between subject and verb = "**The beginning of the good news about Jesus the anointed one—just as it has been written . . . —was John**." (2) The prophecy may represent a subordinate clause to the main clause that follows, in which case ἐγένετο introduces the main or independent clause of the sentence = "**As it has been written in Isaiah . . . , John was baptizing**." This second option would more closely connect the prophecy (in the subordinate clause) with the events being depicted that fulfill the prophecy (in the main clause). (3) Or the preceding prophecy could end the opening sentence, in which case ἐγένετο introduces a new sentence = "**The beginning of the good news . . . [was] just as it is written in Isaiah . . . make his paths level. It was John baptizing in the desert**." Regarding this third scenario, note how the foregrounding of the verb at the beginning of the new sentence enables us to emphasize John as the fulfillment of the prophecy by translating in English, "It (the voice referred to in the prophecy) was John" rather than "John was."

Γίνομαι is a versatile verb that is primarily an equative or linking verb meaning "become" or "was." However, it can also function as an intransitive verb meaning "come" or "happen" or "appear." either of these two syntactical options could be present here. (1) The verb ἐγένετο could function as an equative verb, in which case it could have one of two subjects. The subject of ἐγένετο could be ἀρχή with Ἰωάννης serving as a predicate nominative = "**The beginning of the good news... was John baptizing in the desert.**" Or the subject of ἐγένετο could be Ἰωάννης, in which case ἐγένετο would serve as an equative verb in a periphrastic construction with the participles (βαπτίζων and κηρύσσων) that follow = "**John was baptizing... and [was] proclaiming**" (Decker 6). (2) The verb ἐγένετο could be an intransitive verb denoting an action in its own right (the act of existing), in which case the participles that follow would be circumstantial participles = "**John came baptizing... and proclaiming**" (Williams 21).

- Ἰωάνης nom. sing. masc. of the proper, first declension noun ὁ Ἰωάννης (predicate noun or subject) = "**John.**" Ἰωάννης is either (1) the predicate nominative of a sentence the subject of which is ἀρχή with ἐγένετο as the equative verb (= the beginning was John) or (2) Ἰωάννης is the subject of a sentence whose main verb is ἐγένετο functioning either as an equative verb in a periphrastic construction (="John was baptizing") or an intransitive verb (= "John appeared").

- [ὁ] nom. sing. masc. of the article ὁ, ἡ, τό (signifying an attributive participle or a substantive participle in simple apposition to Ἰωάννης) = "**John who was baptizing**" or "**John, the one baptizing**" (Decker 6).

The unlikely [ὁ] is a textual variant that would change the participle from a predicate adjective in a periphrastic construction or a circumstantial participle into an attributive participle modifying Ἰωάννης or a substantive participle in apposition to Ἰωάννης. The participle would then serve as an epithet, "the baptizer." The awkward result would be: "John the baptizer was in the desert and proclaiming...." However, the more likely syntactical function of βαπτίζων (as a circumstantial participle) prohibits it from serving as an epithet. Only later does Mark refer to John as "the baptist" (ὁ βαπτιστής—6:25; 8:28) or "the baptizer" (6:14, 24) (Williams 21).

- βαπτίζων pres. act. participle nom. sing. masc., of the verb βαπτίζω, agreeing in case, number, and gender with Ἰωάννης (periphrastic participle or a circumstantial participle) = "**John was baptizing**" or "**John

appeared, baptizing." The two options for the syntax of βαπτίζων are: (1) it may be treated as an attributive participle in the present tense forming a periphrasis with the verb ἐγένετο, taken as an equative verb = "**was baptizing.**" The combination of the aorist verb ("was" or "came") with the present participle ("baptizing") has the effect of expressing continuing or repeated action. (2) Or βαπτίζων may be treated as a circumstantial participle to the main verb ἐγένετο, taken as an intransitive verb = "**appeared, baptizing.**" As a circumstantial participle in the present tense, βαπτίζων would express action contemporaneous with the time of the main verb ἐγένετο.

Our preference is to treat the finite verb as transitive and the participle as circumstantial. The use of γίνομαι (rather than εἰμί) may express solemnity (Smyth 1710), a mood in consonance with a gospel announcement and the proclamation of a written prophecy introducing momentous events. The construction is more in the tone of a tragedy rather than a comedy (Smyth 1964). The fact that ἐγένετο is aorist rather than imperfect may also have significance. In this regard, it is interesting that Mark's narrative opens with this aorist and continues the action with so many verbs in the imperfect throughout the narrative.

The word βαπτίζω means to "immerse" or to "dip." Mark uses the word later to refer to the traditions of the elders, who practice "cleansings (baptisms or dippings as a means of purification) for pitchers and cups and copper containers" (7:3-4). The practice of baptism for people took place with converts to Judaism. Here in Mark, baptism is a call for the renewal of Israel in preparation for the arrival of a messianic figure, about whom John is vague ("one stronger than I am").

- ἐν τῇ ἐρήμῳ prepositional phrase (expressing place where) with ἐν + the dative, here the dat. sing. fem. of the (substantive) adjective ἡ ἔρημος (substantive adjective/ dative of place where) = "**in the desert**" or "**in the wilderness**" (Decker 6). This is a verbal thread connecting John's activity with the prophecy Mark has cited from "Isaiah." Together the prophecy and its fulfillment introduce the theme of wilderness/desert in Mark. God can begin new life in a bleak place, with a new cultural and social world emerging from the margins, from a place outside the present culture and society.

καὶ κηρύσσων βάπτισμα μετανοίας εἰς ἄφεσιν ἁμαρτιῶν.

- καί coord. conj. (simple connective for the two participles) = "**and**."
- κηρύσσων pres. act. participle nom, sing. masc. of the verb κηρύσσω, grammatically the same as βαπτίζων and agreeing with Ἰωάνης (an attributive participle in the present tense forming a periphrasis with the main verb ἐγένετο as an equative verb or a circumstantial participle to the main verb ἐγένετο understood as an intransitive verb) = "**and proclaiming**."

Because these two participles are in parallel, the construction suggests that the baptizing and proclaiming do not express a temporal sequence but represent activities going on at the same time. If these two participles are taken as circumstantial participles to the main verb ἐγένετο (understood as an intransitive verb), then it is possible that they express purpose = "**John came in order to baptize . . . and to proclaim**." However, the understanding of κηρύσσων as a circumstantial participle of attendant circumstance is preferable, because the main function of this sentence/clause is not to explain John's purpose but to introduce John as the fulfillment of the prophecy from "Isaiah" that the narrator has just cited.

- βάπτισμα anarthrous acc. sing. neut. of the noun τὸ βάπτισμα (direct object of the participle) = "**a baptism**." Since βάπτισμα is limited by the genitive that follows, it may be possible to consider it as a definite noun = "**the baptism (of repentance)**." Unlike the parallel in 1:1 (Ἀρχὴ τοῦ εὐαγγελίου), however, the genitive here has no definite article.
- μετανοίας gen. fem. sing. of the verbal noun ἡ μετανοία (a genitive of definition identifying what kind of baptism John is proclaiming). Μετανοία is a verbal noun depicting activity (compare the cognate verb μετανοέω). It does not refer to a feeling of sorrow or regret for one's sins, but rather it refers more profoundly to a commitment to turn one's life around, to make a change = "**to change one's understanding**" or "**to turn around**" or "**to repent**" (Williams 21). Here, μετανοίας is equivalent to "confessing one's sins publicly" (see below), so that one can be forgiven and live in a new way. John is calling people to turn *away* from the old life with the result that they will be able to turn *toward* a new life of faith as a response to the rule of God.

John proclaims repentance from the past in preparation for the coming one, but he does not say what will be proclaimed by the coming one. For the moment, it is enough to turn from the past, which also signifies a receptivity to the future coming one. The prophecy Mark has cited (1:2–3) interprets John as one whose actions and proclamation "prepare the way of the Lord." John "baptizes," and he also "proclaims a baptism," showing that his proclamation explains and carries out the meaning of the baptism by calling for repentance and announcing forgiveness.

- εἰς ἄφεσιν prepositional phrase with εἰς + the accusative, here the acc. sing. fem. of the noun ἡ ἄφεσις. (object of the preposition) = "**forgiveness**" or "**pardon**" or "**letting go of**." As a preposition, εἰς expresses movement toward or, in a metaphorical sense, the goal toward which something is moving in terms of purpose, here = "**for (the purpose of) (the) forgiveness**" or "**leading to the pardon of sins**" (Decker 7; Williams 21).

- ἁμαρτιῶν gen. plur. fem. of the noun ἡ ἁμαρτία (an objective genitive, functioning as the object of the implied action of "forgiving" embedded in the verbal noun ἄφεσιν; compare the cognate verb ἀφίημι) = "**[the forgiving] of sins**" (Decker 7).

<1:5> καὶ ἐξεπορεύετο πρὸς αὐτὸν πᾶσα ἡ Ἰουδαία χώρα καὶ οἱ Ἱεροσολυμῖται πάντες, καὶ ἐβαπτίζοντο ὑπ' αὐτοῦ ἐν τῷ Ἰορδάνῃ ποταμῷ ἐξομολογούμενοι τὰς ἁμαρτίας αὐτῶν. = **And the whole Judean countryside was going out to him and all the Jerusalemites, and they were being baptized by him in the Jordan River, confessing publicly their sins.**

καὶ ἐξεπορεύετο πρὸς αὐτὸν πᾶσα ἡ Ἰουδαία χώρα καὶ οἱ Ἱεροσολυμῖται πάντες,

- καί coor. conj. (paratactic, connecting this sentence to the previous one) = "**and**." Beginning the sentence with this conjunction is a common feature of Makan style, and this is the first time it occurs in the gospel (Williams 22).

- ἐξεπορεύετο impf. mid. (in form) ind. 3rd pers. sing. of the deponent verb ἐκπορεύομαι (imperfect of distributive action, depicting the repetition of the same action by different people, as of a stream of people coming out to be baptized) = "**were going out**" (Williams 21). The verb is singular because it agrees with the nearer member (πᾶσα ἡ Ἰουδαία χώρα) of the compound subject (πᾶσα ἡ Ἰουδαία χώρα καὶ οἱ Ἱεροσολυμῖται πάντες) (Smyth 969). Although listed as a "true deponent" by some grammars (i.e., Wallace 430), the verb πορνεύομαι retains the force of its middle voice rather than laying it aside since a subject who goes is necessarily affected by the effects of the going. See comments on the verb γίνομαι in Mark 1:4 above.

- πρός αὐτόν prepositional phrase (expressing motion toward) with πρός + the accusative, here the acc. sing. masc. of the 3rd pers. personal pronoun αὐτός = "**to him**." The antecedent is "John."

- πᾶσα nom. sing. fem. of the pronominal adjective πᾶς (modifying ἡ χώρα in the predicate position) = "**all [the countryside]**." When πᾶς modifies a noun in the attributive position, it signifies the countryside as a "whole" (Smyth 1174a). When πᾶς (as here) modifies a noun in the predicate position, it emphasizes "all" the people who comprise the countryside (Smyth 1174b; Decker 7).

- ἡ ... χώρα nom. sing. fem. of the noun ἡ χώρα (first part of a two-part compound subject) = "**the country**" or "**the countryside**." The word ἡ χώρα refers to a geographical area rather than to the nation as a political entity, although the political dimensions are certainly implied in its use here.

- Ἰουδαία nom. sing. fem. of the adjective Ἰουδαῖος, -η, ον (agrees with χώρα and modifies it as an adjective in the attributive position) = "**all the Judean countryside**." The phrase refers to the rural inhabitants of the agrarian area of Judea around Jerusalem.

- καί coor. conj. (connective, uniting two items that serve as the compound subject of the sentence) = "**and**."

- οἱ Ἱεροσολυμῖται nom. plur. masc. of the first declension masculine noun ὁ Ἱεροσολυμίτης (second part of a two-part compound subject) = "**Jerusalemites or the people of Jerusalem**," referring to residents of Jerusalem.

- πάντες nom. plur. masc. of the pronominal adjective πᾶς (modifying οἱ Ἱεροσολυμῖται in the predicate position) = "**all**." Like πᾶσα above, a pronominal adjective modifying a noun in a predicate position emphasizes all the people who comprise the city = "**all the Jerusalemites**" or "**all the residents of Jerusalem**." Note the parallel between *all* Judea and *all* the Jerusalemites, which together refer to all the peasant farmers and all the city dwellers.

καὶ ἐβαπτίζοντο ὑπ' αὐτοῦ ἐν τῷ Ἰορδάνῃ ποταμῷ

- καί coor. conj. (paratactic, connects this sentence to the previous sentence) = "**and**."
- ἐβαπτίζοντο impf. pass. ind. 3rd pers. plur. of the verb βαπτίζω (distributive imperfect depicting the continuous action of many different people being baptized one after another) = "**were being baptized**" (Decker 7). Although the inclusiveness of the subjects of this verb indicate that all were baptized, Jesus' comments to the chief priests, scribes, and elders in Mark 11:27–33 recognize that not all who came to John believed his proclamation or accepted his baptism (Williams 22).
- ὑπ' αὐτοῦ prepositional phrase (expressing agency) with ὑπό + the genitive, here gen. sing. masc. of the 3rd pers. personal pronoun αὐτός, -ή, -ό (object of the preposition/ genitive of agency) = "**by him (John)**." The preposition ὑπό plus the genitive is the typical way to express "agency of persons" with passive verbs ("agency of things" is usually expressed by the dative of means without a preposition).
- ἐν τῷ Ἰορδάνῃ prepositional phrase (expressing place where) with ἐν + the dative, here the dat, sing, masc. of the first declension noun ἡ Ἰορδάνης (object of the preposition/ dative of place where) = "**in the river Jordan**." The word "Jordan" does not modify "river," because Ἰορδάνῃ is a noun, and nouns do not modify other nouns.
- ποταμῷ dat. sing. masc. of the noun ὁ ποταμός (apposition, being a noun in the same case, as well as the same number and gender, as τῷ Ἰορδάνῃ). The noun ποταμῷ is in apposition to the noun τῷ Ἰορδάνῃ and modifies it by juxtaposition (Smyth 998; Wallace 48–49) = "**Jordan, a river**" or "**the river Jordan**." The phrase could be translated as "the Jordan, [which is] a river" or, by reversing the apposition, "the river Jordan" (Smyth 1142 c).

ἐξομολογούμενοι τὰς ἁμαρτίας αὐτῶν.

- ἐξομολογούμενοι pres. mid. (in form) participle nom. plur. masc. of the verb ἐξομολογέομαι, which agrees grammatically with the implied subject (i. e. "the whole Judean countryside and all the Jerusalemites") of the verb βαπτίζω (circumstantial participle of time contemporaneous with the time of the main verb, clarifying the confessing that accompanied the act of being baptized) = "**confessing**" or (publicly) "**acknowledging**" or (translated as a subordinate temporal clause) "**as they were confessing**" (Williams 23). The prefix ἐκ- has the effect of making the confession public. Because Mark is depicting the baptism of John as a call for the renewal of Israel, we may infer that the sins being confessed include the communal/ corporate sins of the nation. As the narrative progresses, it becomes clear that Mark is seeking to guide readers to break with some core values of the culture (e. g. that greatness is to be equated with power over people).

- τὰς ἁμαρτίας acc. plur. fem. of the noun ἡ ἁμαρτία, (the direct object of the action in the participle ἐξομολογούμενοι) = "**confessing their sins**" or "**publicly acknowledging their sins**."

- αὐτῶν gen. plur. masc. of the third pers. personal pronoun αὐτός (subjective genitive, acting as the subject of the action implied in the verbal noun ἁμαρτία. Compare the cognate verb ἁμαρτάνω) = "**the sinnings by them [those who were being baptized]**" or "**their sins**" (i. e. the sins they have done). The antecedent of this pronoun is "the whole Judean countryside and all the Jerusalemites."

<1:6> **καὶ ἦν ὁ Ἰωάννης ἐνδεδυμένος τρίχας καμήλου καὶ ζώνην δερματίνην περὶ τὴν ὀσφὺν αὐτοῦ, καὶ ἐσθίων ἀκρίδας καὶ μέλι ἄγριον. = and John was wearing camels' hair and (with) a leather belt around his waist and was eating locusts and wild honey.**

καὶ ἦν ὁ Ἰωάννης ἐνδεδυμένος τρίχας καμήλου

- καί coor. conj. (paratactic/ connects this sentence with the previous sentence and introduces new information) = "**and**" or "**now**."

- ὁ Ἰωάννης nom. sing. masc. of the proper noun ὁ Ἰωάννης with an article that is not translated in English (subject) = "**John.**" The function of the article is to point back to the previous reference to John in verse 4 (Smyth 1120a and 1136; Wallace 217–19) = "**Now this John**" (i. e. the one referred to above).

- ἦν ... ἐνδεδυμένος a combination of the imperfect indicative act. 3rd pers. sing. of the equative verb εἰμί and a perf. pass. participle nom. sing. masc. of the verb ἐνδύω that agrees grammatically with the subject ὁ Ἰωάννης (periphrastic construction/ imperfect of habitual action) = "**was dressed in**" (Decker 8–9; Williams 23). Combined with the imperfect of the verb εἰμί, the particle forms a periphrastic construction that may be translated as an imperfect (called a "periphrastic" use of the participle, because it is a round-about way to express the imperfect) = "**was dressed (in)**" or (rendering the passive voice in an active sense) "**was wearing**." In the former translation, the prefix ἐν- allows us to add the English word "in" to the translation. In regard to the latter translation, rendering it in an active voice allows us to see more clearly the function of the direct objects that follow. The equative verb ἦν governs two periphrastic participles: ἐνδεδυμένος and ἐσθίων (see below).

- τρίχας acc. plur. fem. of the noun ἡ θρίξ (first part of a compound direct object) = "**hair**."
- καμήλου gen. sing. masc. of the noun ὁ κάμηλος (partitive genitive with the camel as the whole of which the hair is a part/ or genitive of origin) = "**camel's [hair]**" or "**[hair] from a camel**." The phrase may refer to the untanned skin of a camel or, more likely, a garment made of camel's hair rather than wool.

καὶ ζώνην δερματίνην περὶ τὴν ὀσφὺν αὐτοῦ,

- καί coor. conj. (connective for two direct objects depicting the two different items John is wearing, making it a compound direct object) = "**and**." The connective could be relating the second part of the compound direct object closely to the first part = "**with [a leather belt around his waist]**."
- ζώνην δερματίνην anarthous acc. sing. fem. of the noun ἡ ζώνη modified by the acc. sing. fem. of the adjective δερμάτινος (the second part of the compound direct object of the main verb, paralleling τρίχας καμήλου) = "**a leather belt** or **a leather girdle**." The lack of an article makes the noun indefinite.
- περὶ τὴν ὀσφύν prepositional phrase (expressing place where) with περί + the accusative, here the acc. sing. fem. of the noun ἡ ὀσφύς (object of the preposition) = "**around the waist**."
- αὐτοῦ gen. sing. masc. of the third pers. personal pronoun αὐτός (possessive genitive or partitive genitive in which "he" is the whole of which the "waist" is a part) = "**around the waist of him**" or "**around his waist**." The antecedent of this pronoun is ὁ Ἰωάννης.

καὶ ἐσθίων ἀκρίδας καὶ μέλι ἄγριον.

- καί coor. conj. (connective, connecting the second participle that combines with ἦν (ἐσθίων) to the first participle that combines with ἦν (ἐνδεδυμένος), thereby forming a second periphrastic construction) = "**and**."

- [ἦν . . .] ἐσθίων pres. act. participle nom. sing. masc. of the verb ἐσθίω (in combination with ἦν is an imperfect of habitual action, making it another periphrastic use of the participle) = "**was eating**" (Decker 9; Williams 23). This is the second periphrastic participle governed by the ἦν that occurs at the beginning of the sentence. For an explanation of the periphrastic use of participles, see above under ἦν . . . ἐνδεδυμένος.

- ἀκρίδας acc. plur. fem. of the noun ἡ ἀκρίς (the first part of a two-part compound direct object of the verb ἦν . . . ἐσθίων) = "**locusts**."

- καί coor. conj. (connective for the two direct objects) = "**and**."

- μέλι ἄγριον anarthrous use of the acc. sing. neut. of the noun τὸ μέλι ("honey") modified by the acc. sing. neut. of the adjective ἄγριος, -η, -ον (second part of a compound direct object of the verb ἦν . . . ἐσθίων)= "**wild honey**."

<1:7> καὶ ἐκήρυσσεν λέγων, "Ἔρχεται ὁ ἰσχυρότερός μου ὀπίσω μου, οὗ οὐκ εἰμὶ ἱκανὸς κύψας λῦσαι τὸν ἱμάντα τῶν ὑποδημάτων αὐτοῦ. = **and he was proclaiming, saying, "After me comes one stronger than I, the strap of whose sandals I am not worthy after stooping down to untie."**

καὶ ἐκήρυσσεν λέγων,

- καί coor. conj. (paratactic, connects this verb to the previous periphrastic verb) = "**and**."

- ἐκήρυσσεν impf. act. ind. 3rd pers. sing. of the verb κηρύσσω (either an imperfect of repeated action or an imperfect of customary action) = "**he was preaching**" or "**he would proclaim**."

- λέγων pres. act. participle nom. sing. masc. of the verb λέγω agreeing with the subject ("John") of the main verb (a present circumstantial participle of time concurrent with the time of the main verb) = "**saying**." Λέγων acts to introduce direct speech and can even, when it represents a redundancy (as it does here), be translated simply as a comma and quotation marks (called a recitative λέγων) = , "..." (Decker 9). What follows then is the direct speech of John.

Ἔρχεται ὁ ἰσχυρότερός μου ὀπίσω μου,

- Ἔρχεται pres. mid. (in form) ind. 3rd pers. sing. of the deponent verb ἔρχομαι (a present with future force) = "**is coming**" or "**is going to come**" or "**will come**" (Williams 24). Smyth calls this the present of anticipation (1879, 1881). And Wallace explains that "it typically adds the connotations of immediacy and certainty" (535). Note the use of ἔρχομαι here and elsewhere to express Jesus' sense of purpose and mission. Some grammars list ἔρχομαι as a "true deponent" (i.e., Wallace 430), but the verb retains the force of its middle voice rather than laying it aside since a subject who comes is necessarily affected by the effects of the coming. See comments on the verb γίνομαι in Mark 1:4 above.

- ὁ ἰσχυρότερος nom. sing. masc. form of the adjective ἰσχυρός with a comparative ending -τερος (substantive use of the adjective/ subject) = "**the stronger one**" [is coming].

- μου gen. sing. masc. of the 1st pers. personal pronoun ἐγώ (genitive of comparison after the comparative adjective ἰσχυρότερος) = "**than I [am]**" or "**than me.**" The phrase can best be translated "**[the] one stronger than I [am]**."

- ὀπίσω μου prepositional phrase (expressing subsequent time or place) with ὀπίσω + the genitive, here the gen. sing. masc. of the 1st pers. personal pronoun ἐγώ (object of the preposition) = "**after me.**" This prepositional phrase modifies Ἔρχεται either (1) as an adverb of place (spatially follows after, used as a metaphor, cf. 8:34) or (2), more likely, as an adverb of time (temporally follows after John). Note the use of this Markan phrase in connection with the motif of "following:" Jesus "comes after" John, and the disciples "come after" Jesus (8:34). In 8:34, however, the preposition (as a metaphor) has primarily spatial dimensions, whereas here it has literal temporal semantics.

οὗ οὐκ εἰμὶ ἱκανὸς κύψας λῦσαι τὸν ἱμάντα τῶν ὑποδημάτων αὐτοῦ.

- οὗ gen. sing. masc. of the relative pronoun ὅ (possessive pronoun) = "**whose [strap]**." This pronoun introduces a complex relative clause that needs to be treated as a whole. What follows will first consider the relative clause without the initial relative pronoun, thus treating οὐκ εἰμὶ ἱκανός . . . as a simple sentence. See what follows for further analysis. At the end, we will give a summary.
- εἰμί pres. act. ind. 1st sing of the equative verb εἰμί = "**I am**."
- οὐκ adverbial negative (for verbs in the indicative mood) = **not**. Note the kappa added at the end of οὐ for pronunciation when οὐ precedes words that begin with a vowel and have a soft breathing.
- ἱκανός nom. sing. masc. of the adjective ἱκανός, -ή, -όν in agreement with the subject of the verb εἰμί (a predicate adjective describing the subject) = "**worthy [to]**."
- λῦσαι aor. act. infinitive of the verb λύω (a complementary or epexegetical infinitive after an adjective that takes an infinitive) = "**[worthy] to loose**" or "**to loosen**" (Decker 10; Williams 24). The complementary infinitive gives content to the meaning of the adjective ἱκανός by defining what it is that John is "worthy" to do (or, in this case, "not worthy" to do). On complementary or epexegetical infinitives, see Smyth 2001–2; and Wallace 607.
- κύψας aor. act. participle nom. sing. masc. of the verb κύπτω in grammatical agreement with the unexpressed subject of the infinitive λῦσαι (participle of attendant circumstance or temporal circumstantial participle) = "**to stoop down [and untie]**" or "**after stooping down to untie**."

There are two options for the syntax of the participle κύψας: (1) taken as a participle of attendant circumstance, κύψας expresses an action that is coordinate with the action of the verb to which it is connected (here λῦσαι) (Decker 10). In such a case, it is best translated so as to parallel the grammar of the verb to which it is attached = "**not worthy to stoop down and to untie**." (2) Taken as a temporal circumstantial participle in the aorist, κύψας expresses an action antecedent to the action expressed by the infinitive (Williams 24). It is best translated to show previous action = "**not worthy, after stooping down, to untie**."

The participle κύψας is nominative for the following reason. When the subject of the infinitive is the same as the subject of the governing verb (as it is here), the subject of the infinitive is not expressed, and any modifiers of this unexpressed subject stand in the nominative case (Smyth 1973; Williams 192). Therefore, κύψας is in the nominative case, agreeing with the unexpressed subject of the infinitive, which is in the nominative.

- τὸν ἱμάντα acc. sing. masc. of the noun ὁ ἱμάς (direct object of the infinitive λῦσαι) = "**the strap**."
- τῶν ὑποδημάτων gen. plur. neut. of the noun τὸ ὑπόδημα (a partitive genitive in which the sandals are the whole of which the strap is a part) = "**of the sandals**."
- αὐτοῦ gen. sing. masc. of the 3rd pers. personal pronoun αὐτός (possessive genitive limiting the noun ὑποδημάτων) = "**his [sandals]**." The antecedent of this pronoun is ὁ ἰσχυρότερος.

So far, we have treated the sentence that makes up the clause. Now consider the clause along with the initial relative pronoun. The relative pronoun οὗ (gen. sing. masc.) at the beginning of the clause agrees in number and gender with its antecedent (ὁ ἰσχυρότερός) but it has the genitive case as a means to serve its syntactical function in the relative clause—a possessive genitive. This possessive genitive may go with one of two words in the sentence: (1) It may relate to τῶν ὑποδημάτων, in which case the relative possessive οὗ is repeated by αὐτοῦ (= "the strap of whose sandals of his"). In this syntactical scenario, the redundant pleonasm αὐτοῦ is not translated, and the clause would read = "**the strap of whose (his) sandals I am not worthy after stooping down to untie**." Or (2), the relative possessive may go with τὸν ἱμάντα, in which case the translation would be = "**whose strap of his sandal I am not worthy after stooping down to untie**." In either case, the clause emphasizes that John is not worthy of doing the lowliest task of a slave in relation to the greatness of the stronger one coming after him.

<1:8> ἐγὼ ἐβάπτισα ὑμᾶς ὕδατι, αὐτὸς δὲ βαπτίσει ὑμᾶς ἐν πνεύματι ἁγίῳ. = "**I baptized you with water, but he will baptize you in (the) holy spirit**."

ἐγὼ ἐβάπτισα ὑμᾶς ὕδατι

- ἐγώ nom. sing. of the 1st pers. personal pronoun ἐγώ (emphatic nominative) = "**I**" or "**I myself**." The contrast with the following parallel clause ("in water . . . , but he . . .") may be adequate to express the emphatic pronoun in English (Decker 10; Williams 24).

- ἐβάπτισα aor. act. ind. 1st pers. sing. of the verb βαπτίζω (a global aorist expressing all the separate baptisms together as a single act) = "**I baptized**" (Decker 11).
- ὑμᾶς acc. plur. of the 2nd pers. personal pronoun σύ (direct object) = "**you**" (plural).
- ὕδατι dat. sing. of the noun τὸ ὕδωρ (a dative of means) = "**with water.**" Or it could be a locative dative of place or a dative of sphere = "**in water**" (Decker 11).

αὐτὸς δὲ βαπτίσει ὑμᾶς

- δέ postpositive coor. conj. (adversative) = "**but**" or "**by contrast.**"
- αὐτός nom. sing. masc. of the 3rd pers. masc. personal pronoun αὐτός (emphatic pronoun paralleling ἐγώ in the clause above) = "**he**" or "**he himself.**"
- βαπτίσει fut. act. ind. 3rd pers. sing. of the verb βαπτίζω (a global, predictive or prophetic future covering collectively all the acts of this kind of baptism in the future) = "**he will baptize.**" The contrast between a present baptism of water and an impending baptism of holy spirit may suggest that, for Mark, a baptism of water is no longer in force when John's activity comes to an end.
- ὑμᾶς acc. plur. of the 2nd pers. personal pronoun (direct object, paralleling the direct object of the first clause) = "**you**" (plural).
- ἐν πνεύματι ἁγίῳ prepositional phrase (expressing means) with ἐν + the dative, here dat. sing. neut. of the noun τὸ πνεῦμα modified by dat. sing. neut. of the adjective ἅγιος (object of the preposition/ dative of means) = "**with [the] holy spirit**" or "**in the Holy Spirit.**" This dative of means or instrument following the preposition would function in the same way without the preposition ἐν, similar to ὕδατι in the first clause. The preposition ἐν plus the dative could express the same sense of instrumentality understood as a dative of personal agency. Or the dative could be taken as a dative of sphere = "**in holy spirit.**" Such an interpretation would parallel the immersion in water with a metaphorical immersion in the power of the spirit.

In Mark's Gospel, the baptism in holy spirit does not have the meaning that it does in the Acts of the Apostles, where people have an ecstatic experience of the spirit and speak in tongues. Rather, in Mark, the experience of being healed or exorcized by one who is endowed with the spirit may be the baptism of which John speaks. Also, in Mark, Jesus prophesies that the holy spirit will give people the words to speak when they are called to witness amid persecution (13:11). As such, for Mark, the baptism of the spirit may be a baptism of suffering, because Jesus refers to death by persecution as a baptism (10:35–40).

Note also that, in Mark's portrayal, there is nothing in what John says or does to suggest that John knows the actual identity of the one about whom he is prophesying. John predicts that another figure is coming after him, that this stronger one is much greater than he (John) and that this one will baptize in holy spirit—but there is no indication that John knows that Jesus is the one coming.

WHAT FOLLOWS

What follows this passage is the appearance of Jesus as the fulfillment of John's prophecies. Just as Isaiah prophesied and John appeared to fulfill Isaiah's prophecy, so now John has prophesied, and Jesus appears on the scene to fulfill that prophesy—and much more. The narrative so far has served to set the readers up to respond to Jesus as a reliable character from whom they can expect great things. In the episode that follows, God adds further credibility to Jesus by ripping open the heavens, sending the spirit upon him, and declaring him to be God's son. By the time Jesus emerges publicly to proclaim the rule of God and to call disciples, we readers are prepared to trust him and respond to his message.

2

The Baptism and The Temptation of Jesus

Mark 1:9–13

PREVIEW

These two episodes focus on the baptism and temptation of Jesus. The previous episode ends with the narrator introducing John's baptism and his proclamation about the one coming after him. Now the narrator depicts Jesus' baptism by John. Note how the two episodes of Jesus' baptism and temptation are held together with the previous episode by John's prophecy and Jesus' fulfillment, by the repetition of key words, and by depicting Jesus' baptism as part of the larger movement of baptism for the renewal of Israel. Nevertheless, Jesus' baptism is clearly different from that of others: the heavens open, the spirit descends upon him, and a voice from heaven declares him to be God's son. All of this makes the baptism of Jesus by John also a royal anointing by God, which, as the subsequent narrative shows, prepares Jesus to be God's agent who will announce the arrival of the rule of God. In the narrative that follows, events move quickly (εὐθύς). Just after his anointing as son of God, Jesus is immediately driven by the spirit into the desert to be tested by Satan for forty days. Clearly, he triumphs in this testing, because he can be with the wild animals (with no harm done to him) and because angels serve him.

‹1:9› Καὶ ἐγένετο ἐν ἐκείναις ταῖς ἡμέραις
ἦλθεν Ἰησοῦς ἀπὸ Ναζαρὲτ τῆς Γαλιλαίας
   καὶ ἐβαπτίσθη εἰς τὸν Ἰορδάνην ὑπὸ Ἰωάννου.
‹1:10› καὶ εὐθὺς ἀναβαίνων ἐκ τοῦ ὕδατος

εἶδεν σχιζομένους τοὺς οὐρανοὺς
   καὶ τὸ πνεῦμα ὡς περιστερὰν ·
     καταβαῖνον εἰς αὐτόν·
‹1:11› καὶ φωνὴ ἐγένετο ἐκ τῶν οὐρανῶν,
   Σὺ εἶ ὁ υἱός μου ὁ ἀγαπητός,
   ἐν σοὶ εὐδόκησα.
‹1:12› Καὶ εὐθὺς τὸ πνεῦμα αὐτὸν ἐκβάλλει
εἰς τὴν ἔρημον.
‹1:13› καὶ ἦν ἐν τῇ ἐρήμῳ τεσσεράκοντα ἡμέρας
   πειραζόμενος ὑπὸ τοῦ Σατανᾶ,
καὶ ἦν μετὰ τῶν θηρίων,
   καὶ οἱ ἄγγελοι διηκόνουν αὐτῷ.

And it happened in those days (that) Jesus came from Nazareth of the Galilee
   and <u>was baptized</u> <u>in the Jordan</u> <u>by John</u>.
And immediately (as he was) <u>coming up from the water</u>

he saw <u>the heavens</u> being ripped apart
   and the <u>spirit</u> like a dove
     <u>coming</u> down onto him.
And a voice came from <u>the heavens</u>,
   "<u>You</u> are my beloved son;
   I was delighted by <u>you</u>."
And immediately <u>the spirit</u> drives him out
into <u>the desert</u>.
And he was in <u>the desert</u> forty days
   being tested by Satan,
and he was with wild animals
   and the angels were serving him.

MARKAN WORD FIELDS

There are several word fields in this passage. The overarching word field is that of (1) "prophecy and fulfillment:" John fulfills Isaiah's prophecy and Jesus fulfills John's prophecy. Embedded in the description of John as the fulfillment of prophecy is the word field of (2) "baptism." The description of Jesus' baptism is also related to the word field of (3) "anointing a king." Embedded within Jesus' anointing are two minor word fields: (4) "cosmic manifestations" and (5) "vision/audition experiences." Finally, the rhetoric of the passage manifests "concealing/revealing" dynamics and the word field of "temptation."

The Baptism and The Temptation of Jesus

"Prophecy and Fulfillment"

The sequence of events in this episode is a continuing part of the first word field of the Gospel that began with Isaiah's prophecy. Isaiah prophesies and John fulfills the prophecy. Then John prophesies and Jesus fulfills the prophecy. Later, Jesus will prophesy about the end of his own life and about events that the disciples will fulfill.

Prophecies are driving forces in Mark's narrative, for prophetic oracles not only presage events but also serve to generate them. Prophecy and fulfillment provide many of the verbal threads that weave this narrative together through foreshadowing and retrospection, anticipation and echoes, cause and effect. From the beginning, therefore, the reader comes to expect that prophecies uttered within the narrative will have their fulfillment in events subsequently depicted in the narrative. As a result, the reader comes to trust that all prophecies given by Jesus will be fulfilled, even when their fulfillment is not narrated but is projected into the future of the story world.

The narrative portrays John as the one who fulfills Isaiah's prophecy: John is the "messenger" who is "crying out" and who does so "in the desert." Isaiah's prophecy involved (1) preparation and (2) proclamation. Both aspects of what John does are a fulfillment of Isaiah's prophecy: (1) John urges the people to prepare by participating in a "baptism of repentance" (βάπτισμα μετανοίας) leading to "the pardoning of sins" (εἰς ἄφεσιν ἁμαρτιῶν), and (2) John proclaims the superior strength of "the one coming after me" (ὁ ἰσχυρότερός μου ὀπίσω μου) who "will baptize you in holy spirit" (αὐτὸς δὲ βαπτίσει ὑμᾶς ἐν πνεύματι ἁγίῳ).

Isaiah had prophesied a preparation of the roads across the desert from Babylon to Israel in Palestine. In the story, John fulfills the prophecy in a metaphorical way. This is preparation for the coming of God by the agent who will represent him. Preparation for the coming rule of God involves not the repairing of roads but the removal of sins, for it is sin that would keep the people from receiving and responding to the rulership of the holy God over the world. Because Mark portrays John's baptism as a renewal of Israel, the confession implied here relates primarily to the corporate sins of the nation.

Then Jesus comes from Nazareth of Galilee and is baptized by John in the Jordan. The fulfillment parallels (in reverse) the two points of John's prophecy: (2) the spirit comes upon Jesus as an anointing that will enable him to "baptize you with holy spirit," and (1) Jesus is shown to be greater than John, demonstrated by the voice of God announcing Jesus as God's son. The complete fulfillment of John's prophecy will come throughout the subsequent narrative as Jesus (1) demonstrates his worthiness to be "son of God" and (2) baptizes people with holy spirit through healing, exorcism, and the sharing of authority with disciples, among other things.

"Anointing of a King"

When Jesus is baptized with water, he receives the spirit. In addition to a baptism with water by John, therefore, Jesus' baptism is an anointing with the spirit by God. We have said that Isaiah and John were announcing the arrival of a leader who would inaugurate the coming rule of God. Here we have the anointing of God's agent Jesus to announce and establish that rule of God.

This anointing is like the anointing of a political king in Israel, but it is also very different. It occurs in conjunction with a baptism of repentance for pardon of sins for the people. The heavens are opened (σχιζομένους τοὺς οὐρανοὺς) and the spirit comes upon Jesus, as a dove might descend and alight on someone (καὶ τὸ πνεῦμα ὡς περιστερὰν καταβαῖνον εἰς αὐτόν). Then there is a voice from heaven (καὶ φωνὴ ἐγένετο ἐκ τῶν οὐρανῶν). The voice from God has two parts. The first part (from an enthronement Psalm) establishes Jesus as the definitive agent of God (Σὺ εἶ ὁ υἱός μου ὁ ἀγαπητός) and the second part (from the servant song of Second Isaiah) indicates the kind of servant-messiah this agent of God will be (ἐν σοὶ εὐδόκησα).

"Cosmic Manifestations" and "Vision/Audition"

Embedded in the description of Jesus' baptism/anointing, two minor word fields occur that serve to establish Jesus as the "anointed one, the son of God." The first minor word field depicts cosmic events: "the heavens are split," "the spirit descends," and "a voice comes from heaven." The other word field is the complement of this, whereby Jesus experiences these cosmic events in a vision and an audition: Jesus "saw" the heavens ripped apart and the spirit coming upon him and he hears the voice from heaven. Jesus experiences these things happening as an anointing for the royal mission to follow.

The Baptism and The Temptation of Jesus

"Concealment and Revealing"

The events in this episode both reveal and conceal. Note the difference between what the readers know and what the characters in the story (do not) know. The readers know that John's activity fulfills John's prophecy. The people in the story who come to be baptized by John do not know that his baptism is a fulfillment of prophecy. The readers know that Jesus sees the heavens opened and the spirit descending and the readers know what God has spoken from heaven. But no other characters in the story, apart from Jesus, know this. Jesus has a private vision of these cosmic events. Jesus alone sees the spirit (εἶδεν) and the voice is directed to him (σοι), and no other characters see or hear what Jesus sees and hears. John does not know that the one he has prophesied about has come for baptism. The crowds do not know that Jesus has had a vision and heard a voice. Later, it becomes apparent that no one (except the demons), not even the disciples, know that Jesus is the one anointed by God to inaugurate God's rule. Eventually the disciples will recognize who Jesus is. However, the reader is in on the experience from the beginning. These early events (to which the readers are privy) make clear to the readers that Jesus is indeed the anointed one the son of God, the one for whom preparation is required, the one about whom John has prophesied—this one is about to arrive on the public scene.

"Temptation"

The language of the temptation scene recalls Israel's temptation in the wilderness—"in the desert" "for forty days." Jesus recapitulates the experiences of Israel and succeeds whereas Israel failed. That he succeeds is shown by his emergence to announce that "the rule of God has arrived." The idea that the events here are significant for all creation is shown by the presence of wild beasts (which pose no threat to Jesus) and the angels who "serve" him.

"The Rule of God"

The overarching word field for Mark's story is the establishment of the rule of God over the cosmos. In this episode, the language fields show Jesus as the agent to usher in God's rule. Soon Jesus will announce the arrival of the rule of God.

STRUCTURE

The structure of this section needs to be seen in the context of the whole prologue (1:1–15). We have included below an analysis that accounts for John's baptizing, Jesus' baptism, and the temptation (Noble 379). As we have seen, one structural pattern is that of prophecy and fulfillment: Isaiah's prophecy (1:2–3); the fulfillment (1:4–8); John's prophecy (1:7–9); the fulfillment (1:9–11).

Another pattern of structure begins with the introduction of John and gradually transfers the focus of the narrative from John to Jesus and the proclamation of the rule of God. Each element is essential for the next event to happen: (1) the prophecy of Isaiah leads to the appearance of John; (2) John's preparation of the people and the proclamation of one coming after him leads to Jesus' baptism; (3) the baptism/anointing of Jesus leads the spirit to drive him into the desert to confront Satan; and (4) only after the anointing by God and the triumph over Satan is Jesus able to announce that "the rule of God has arrived." These events correspond to the basic narrative units of the prologue. What is helpful about noticing this structure is that one can attend to the ways in which each unit leads logically and necessarily to the next unit.

Situation

    Setting

    <1:4> John appeared baptizing in the desert   a
    and proclaiming a baptism of repentance for the pardon of sins.   b

    Situation

    <1:5> And going out to him were all the Judean countryside
    and all the Jerusalemites,

    Reply to the situation   a
    and they were being baptized by him in the Jordan River
    acknowledging publicly their sins.

Reply to the situation

    Situation

    <1:6> Now John was dressed in camel's hair
        with a leather belt around his waist
    and was eating locusts and wild honey.

The Baptism and The Temptation of Jesus

Reply to the situation   b
<1:7> And he was proclaiming (saying),
    "After me comes the one stronger than I am;   a
        I am not worthy to stoop (down)   b
and untie the straps of his sandals.
    <1:8> I baptized you with water,   b
    but he will baptize you with holy spirit."   a

Setting
    <1:9> And it happened in those days (that)
        Jesus came from Nazareth of the Galilee
        and was baptized in the Jordan by John.

Situation

  Setting
  <1:10> And immediately (as he was) coming up from the water

  Situation
    he saw the heavens being ripped apart   a
  and the spirit like a dove coming down onto him.   b

Reply to the situation

  Reply to the situation
  <1:11> And a voice came from the heavens,   a
    "You are my beloved son;
    I was delighted by you."

Consequence

  Setting
  <1:12> And immediately the spirit drove him into the desert.   b

  Situation
  <1:13> And he was in the desert forty days   a
        tempted by Satan.   b
    And he was with the wild beasts   a

  Reply to the situation
  and the angels were serving him.   b

Finally, note the parallels suggested by the ab ab patterns. The introduction of John as (a) baptizing and (b) proclaiming corresponds to the subsequent description of John, (a) first of his baptism and (b) then of his proclaiming.

These parallels make clear the two-fold nature of John's mission. Furthermore, the abba pattern within the proclamation itself (7–8) clarifies the basis for saying that John is inferior, namely because John baptized with water whereas Jesus will baptize with holy spirit. So it is the holy spirit that will make Jesus more powerful than John.

In the parallels of Jesus' baptism, the introduction to (a) the opening of the heavens and (b) the descent of the spirit correspond (a) to the subsequent voice that comes from the heavens and (b) to the activity of the spirit in driving Jesus into the desert. Finally, the pattern in the description of the temptation correlates (a) the experience of being in the desert with (a) being among wild beast, and it correlates (b) the testing by Satan with (b) the support Jesus receives from the angels. Parallel patterns such as these help us to see how one or more lines in the Gospel helps to illuminate and interpret other lines by showing which lines and sequences go together.

LINGUISTIC COMMENTARY

<1:9> Καὶ ἐγένετο ἐν ἐκείναις ταῖς ἡμέραις ἦλθεν Ἰησοῦς ἀπὸ Ναζαρὲτ τῆς Γαλιλαίας καὶ ἐβαπτίσθη εἰς τὸν Ἰορδάνην ὑπὸ Ἰωάννου. = **And it happened in those days (that) Jesus came from Nazareth of Galilee and was baptized in the Jordan by John.**

Καὶ ἐγένετο ἐν ἐκείναις ταῖς ἡμέραις

- Καί coor. conj. (paratactic, connects this sentence to the previous sentence) = "**and.**"

- ἐγένετο aor. mid. (in form) ind. 3rd. pers. sing. of the deponent verb γίνομαι = "**it happened.**" This construction (ἐγένετο ἐν ἐκείναις ταῖς ἡμέραις) together with ἦλθεν (see below) is not standard Greek but represents semitic influence (Decker 12). Hebrew prose narrative often places a temporal reference in an independent clause at the beginning of the sentence and then juxtaposes it asyndetically (without a connective) with another main clause that carries the narrative forward. For similar examples in Mark, see 2:15, 23 and 4:4. For a critique of the verb γίνομαι as deponent, see the commentary on Mark 1:4.

- ἐν (ἐκείναις) ταῖς ἡμέραις prepositional phrase with ἐν + the dative, here dat. plur. fem. of ἡ ἡμέρα (object of the preposition/ dative of time when) = "**in the days**."
- ἐκείναις dat. plur. fem. of the demonstrative pronoun ἐκεῖνος, -η, -ο (designating distance) modifying ταῖς ἡμέραις (demonstrative pronouns modify nouns in the predicate position) = "**in those days**." As with other substantives, the demonstrative pronoun can modify another substantive by juxtaposition, which was the original way Greek marked modification.

ἦλθεν Ἰησοῦς ἀπὸ Ναζαρὲτ τῆς Γαλιλαίας

- ἦλθεν 2nd aor. act. ind 3rd. pers. sing. of the deponent verb ἔρχομαι (punctiliar aorist) = "**he (Jesus) came**." In contrast to the predominance of the imperfect tenses in the previous section, the aorist dominates here. Mark presents Jesus' baptism as a series of definite discrete actions. The ordinary word ἔρχομαι has extraordinary meaning in relation to Jesus' mission in Mark. See, for example, 1:39 and 2:17. Most grammars consider ἔρχομαι as a deponent verb, but it has active forms in the third and fourth principal parts, and so ἦλθεν is an active form and not deponent (Wallace 430). See the explanation of the so-called deponency of this verb in Mark 1:7.
- Ἰησοῦς nom. sing. masc. of the proper name ὁ Ἰησοῦς (subject) = "**Jesus**." This is the only time in Mark's Gospel that this name occurs without the definite article, but this is also the first time this name appears in the Gospel aside from this Gospel's title in Mark 1:1 (Decker 12). The definite article with this name in subsequent occurrences points back to this first usage of the name (Smyth 1136).
- ἀπὸ Ναζαρὲτ prepositional phrase with ἀπό + the genitive, here the gen. sing. fem. of the noun ἡ Ναζαρέτ (object of the preposition/ genitive of origin) = "**from Nazareth**." As a proper noun and name, Ναζαρέτ is not declined in the genitive. The prepositional phrase ἀπὸ Ναζαρέτ can modify either the verb or the subject. (1) If it modifies the verb ἦλθεν, it means that Jesus came/traveled from Nazareth = "**Jesus came from Nazareth**" (Decker 12). (2) If it links to the noun Jesus, it identifies Jesus as a citizen of Nazareth = "**Jesus from (a citizen of) Nazareth of Galilee came and was baptized**." Introductions in the Hellenistic world usually stated a person's citizenship by means of a

prepositional phrase with ἀπό or ἐκ + the place of origin (e. g. Tobit 1:1).

- τῆς Γαλιλαίας gen. sing. fem. of the proper name ἡ Γαλιλαία (partitive genitive in which τῆς Γαλιλαίας is the whole of which the city of Ναζαρέτ is a part) = **"from Nazareth of (in) Galilee."**

καὶ ἐβαπτίσθη εἰς τὸν Ἰορδάνην ὑπὸ Ἰωάννου.

- καί coor. conj. (paratactic, connects the two verbs ἦλθεν and ἐβαπτίσθη) = **"and."**
- ἐβαπτίσθη aor. pass. ind. 3rd pers. sing. of the verb βαπτίζω (punctiliar aorist) = **"was baptized."**
- εἰς τὸν Ἰορδάνην prepositional phrase (expressing motion toward and into) with εἰς + the accusative, here the acc. sing. masc. of the proper noun ὁ Ἰορδάνης (object of the preposition) = **"in the Jordan."** Note that the phrase represents a plunging movement "into the Jordan (River)" or at minimum (with εἰς equal to ἐν) an immersion "in the Jordan."
- ὑπὸ Ἰωάννου prepositional phrase with ὑπό + the genitive, here gen. sing. masc. of the proper name ὁ Ἰωάννης (object of the preposition/ genitive of agency) = **"by John."** With verbs in the passive voice, impersonal agency is expressed by the dative of means without a preposition, whereas personal agency, as here, is expressed by ὑπό plus the genitive of agency (Smyth 1491–94; Wallace 431–35).

<1:10> καὶ εὐθὺς ἀναβαίνων ἐκ τοῦ ὕδατος εἶδεν σχιζομένους τοὺς οὐρανοὺς καὶ τὸ πνεῦμα ὡς περιστερὰν καταβαῖνον εἰς αὐτόν· = **And immediately coming up from the water, he saw the heavens being ripped open and the spirit like a dove coming down onto him.**

καὶ εὐθὺς ἀναβαίνων ἐκ τοῦ ὕδατος

- καί coor. conj. (paratactic, connecting this sentence to the previous one) = **"and."**
- εὐθύς adverb of time modifying the main verb εἶδεν = **"immediately."**

- ἀναβαίνων pres. act. participle nom, sing. masc. of the verb ἀναβαίνω (present circumstantial participle of time concurrent with the time of the main verb) = "**coming up**" or "**as he was coming up**."
- ἐκ τοῦ ὕδατος prepositional phrase with ἐκ + the genitive, here gen. sing. neut. of the noun τὸ ὕδωρ (object of the preposition/ genitive of origin) = "**out of the water**" or "**from the water**."

εἶδεν σχιζομένους τοὺς οὐρανούς

- εἶδεν 2nd aor. act. ind. 3rd pers. sing. of the verb ὁράω (punctiliar aorist) = "**he saw**." What follows is a private vision and audition that Jesus himself has. This verb indicates that Jesus "sees" neither simply with his eyes nor as a spectator but as a participant in the unfolding action.
- τοὺς οὐρανούς acc. plur. masc. of the noun ὁ οὐρανός (direct object) = "**the heavens**." It is not uncommon for the plural "heavens" to be used to refer to the sky or as an equivalent to the singular "heaven." At the same time, ancient cosmology did imagine levels or layers of heavens, beginning from the earth up to where God dwelled. In that regard, the plural may suggest that all the levels of heaven are ripped open so no barrier remains between God (in the seventh or uppermost heaven) and Jesus. Σχιζομένους (see below) is the same verb used in 15:38 to describe the ripping of the curtain in the temple that separated God from humans. In Mark's presentation, both Jesus' life and his death open up access to God.
- σχιζομένους pres. mid. or pass. participle acc. plur. masc. of the verb σχίζω (circumstantial participle of time, expressing action contemporaneous with the time of the main verb or a supplementary participle) = "**being ripped apart**" or **being opened**" or "**as it was being ripped open**." As a present circumstantial participle of time, the verb describes what Jesus saw "as he was coming up from the water." A supplemental participle is used with a verb of physical perception and states the action that is seen (Williams 25). The supplementary participle as such denotes actual physical perception (Smyth 2110; Wallace 645–46). We know the participle σχιζομένους refers to "the heavens" because its grammatical identification agrees with τοὺς οὐρανούς. The position of σχιζομένους before τοὺς οὐρανούς places emphasis on the action of ripping. Note again, as mentioned above, that this is the same word used of the rending of the curtain in the sanctuary (15:38).

A LINGUISTIC MODEL TO ANALYZE NEW TESTAMENT GREEK

In both cases, the ripping is followed by a declaration (revelation) that Jesus is God's son (Williams 25).

καὶ τὸ πνεῦμα ὡς περιστερὰν καταβαῖνον εἰς αὐτόν·

- καί coor. conj. (simple connective, connects the two direct objects governed by the verb εἶδεν) = "**and**."
- τὸ πνεῦμα acc. sing. neut. of the noun τὸ πνεῦμα (direct object) = "**the spirit**." Note that the word "holy" is not used here to modify "spirit," but, obviously, based on John's prophecy, it is implied that this is the holy spirit.
- ὡς correlative adverb of comparison (ὡς plus a noun of comparison) = "**as**" or "**like**."
- περιστεράν acc. sing. fem. of the noun ἡ περιστερά agreeing in case and number but not gender with τὸ πνεῦμα = "**a dove**."

There are two ways to take the phrase ὡς περιστεράν (Decker 13–14). (1) The phrase ὡς περιστεράν may be seen as an adverbial phrase of comparison. (a) The comparison may connect to the noun τὸ πνεῦμα, depicting the appearance of the spirit = "**(looking) like a dove**." (b) More likely, this adverbial phrase may modify the participle καταβαῖνον, in which case the comparison is with the manner in which the spirit came down = "**descending like a dove**." An analogy with the action of a dove may also control the meaning of εἰς as "onto" rather than "into," even though there is every implication in either case that the spirit remained upon Jesus and entered into him.

(2) The phrase ὡς περιστεράν may also be taken as a correlative adverb with the semantics of manner and the syntax of a relative clause (Smyth 2462–63; Wallace 761–62) = "**descending as a dove [descends]**." The subject of a ὡς clause is nominative but often attracted to the case of the other member of the comparison, especially when the other member is accusative and the verb is elided from the ὡς clause as it is here (Smyth 2465). Thus, while περιστεράν is the subject of the ὡς clause, it is attracted to the accusative case of τὸ πνεῦμα.

- καταβαῖνον pres. act. participle acc. sing. neut. of the verb καταβαίνω (agreeing with τὸ πνεῦμα and functioning just as σχιζομένους does above, a present circumstantial participle of time expressing action contemporaneous with the time of the main verb and describing the action of the spirit and/or a supplementary participle) = "**coming down.**" A supplementary participle expresses action perceived. The accusative noun τὸ πνεῦμα describes the object seen, while the participle καταβαῖνον describes the action seen. We know that the two participles in this sentence (σχιζομένους and καταβαῖνον) are circumstantial/supplementary and not attributive, because they do not modify their related nouns in an attributive position (contra Decker 14).

- εἰς αὐτόν prepositional phrase of motion toward or into, with εἰς + the accusative, here the acc. sing. masc. of the 3rd person personal pronoun αὐτός (object of the preposition) = "**onto him**" or "**upon him**" or "**into him.**" The metaphor makes the most sense when we think of a dove coming "onto" him. But the implication of the story is that the spirit went "into" him. The depiction of the spirit's coming "into" Jesus at his baptism provides an interesting contrast to the depiction of the spirit's going "out of" him at his death (15:37).

Note again that all of this action has been depicted as a private vision of Jesus: "*he* saw" the heavens being ripped apart and the spirit coming down as a dove.

<1:11> καὶ φωνὴ ἐγένετο ἐκ τῶν οὐρανῶν, Σὺ εἶ ὁ υἱός μου ὁ ἀγαπητός, ἐν σοὶ εὐδόκησα. = **and a voice came from the heavens, "*You* are my beloved son; I was delighted by you."**

καὶ φωνὴ ἐγένετο ἐκ τῶν οὐρανῶν,

- καί coor. conj. (paratactic, connects this sentence to the previous one) = "**and.**"
- φωνή nom. sing. fem. of the verb ἡ φωνή (subject) = "**a voice.**"
- ἐγένετο aor. mid. (in form) ind. 3rd pers. sing. of the deponent verb γίνομαι (punctiliar aorist) = "**came**" (Williams 25). The verb ἐγένετο can function as an equative verb (= was) or as an intransitive verb (= came, appeared). Here, ἐγένετο means "came" rather than "was," due to its relation to the prepositional phrase that follows ("A voice came from . . ."). In this context, ἐγένετο might even mean "sounded forth" (BDAG γίνομαι I. 4. c. β). For this verb as a so-called deponent, see the commentary on Mark 1:4.

- ἐκ τῶν οὐρανῶν prepositional phrase with ἐκ + the genitive, here gen. plur. masc. of the noun ὁ οὐρανός (object of the preposition/ genitive of source) = "**from the heavens**." What follows are the words of the voice. On the plural form of τῶν οὐρανῶν, see the comments on 1:10 above.

Σὺ εἶ ὁ υἱός μου ὁ ἀγαπητός,

- Σύ nom. sing. of the 2nd person personal pronoun σύ (emphatic nominative) = "**you**" (emphatic). The emphatic use of the personal pronoun conveys the meaning "you yourself" or "you, in contrast to all others." The second person singular pronoun here (σύ) and below (σοί) makes it clear that God is addressing Jesus privately and that Jesus is the only one who hears the voice.
- εἶ pres. act. ind. 2nd pers. sing. of the equative verb εἰμί = "**you are**."
- ὁ υἱός nom. sing. masc. of the noun ὁ υἱός (a predicate noun in the nominative case agrees grammatically with the subject) = "**the son**.
- μου gen. sing. of the 1st person personal pronoun ἐγώ (genitive of relationship) = "**my** [son]." The pronoun stands between the noun and the adjective that follows it.
- ὁ ἀγαπητός nom. sing. masc. of the adjective ἀγαπητός, -ή, όν (modifies in an attributive position) = (literally) "**beloved**" or (by common usage) "**only**." The whole phrase can be rendered "my beloved son" or "my son the loved (one)" or "my only son." This adjective is used by Greek speakers in reference to an only child. If a parent has more than one child, then neither can be beloved because they must share the parent's love whereas an only child receives the exclusive love of the parent and is the beloved child.

ἐν σοὶ εὐδόκησα.

- ἐν σοί prepositional phrase with ἐν + the dative, here the dat. sing. of the 2nd person personal pronoun σύ (object of the preposition/dative of respect) = "**with respect to you**" or "**in you**" or "**by you**."
- εὐδόκησα aor. act. ind. 1st pers. sing. of the verb εὐδοκέω. There are several ways to interpret the syntactical use of the aorist (Williams 25–26; Decker 14). (1) The aorist may be a punctiliar aorist = "**I delighted in**

you" (at the moment I chose you). (2) It may be a global aorist = "**I was delighted by you**" (throughout the time before I chose you) (3) It may be an inceptive aorist, which would fit the context of the coronation of a king (see Ps. 2:7) = "**I am delighting in you**" (starting now). (4) Or it could refer to God's choice itself as in the common English phrase "what is your pleasure" = "**I was pleased to choose you**" (just now when the heavens were opened and the spirit descended on you).

Again, note the assumption that, just as the action of ripping and the descent of the spirit were part of a private vision of Jesus, so also these words of God in turn are a private audition for Jesus. In Mark's narrative, no one, neither John nor the people who have come for baptism, know that Jesus is the messiah, nor do they know that anyone has been so anointed as Jesus was at this baptism. Within the story world, that information or experience was not available to them. At this point in the narrative, only Jesus (and the reader) knows that he is "the messiah, the son of God" (1:1).

<1:12> Καὶ εὐθὺς τὸ πνεῦμα αὐτὸν ἐκβάλλει εἰς τὴν ἔρημον. = **And immediately the spirit drives him out into the desert.**

Καὶ εὐθὺς τὸ πνεῦμα αὐτὸν ἐκβάλλει εἰς τὴν ἔρημον.

- Καὶ is a coor. conj. (paratactic) = "**and.**"
- εὐθὺς is an adverb of time modifying ἐκβάλλει = "**at once**" or "**immediately.**"
- τὸ πνεῦμα is nom. sing. neut. of τὸ πνεῦμα (subject) = "**the spirit.**"
- αὐτὸν is acc. sing. masc. of the 3rd person pronoun αὐτός (direct object) = "**him** (Jesus)."
- ἐκβάλλει is pres. act. ind. 3rd pers. sing. of ἐκβάλλω (historical present) = "[the spirit] "**drives [him] out**" or "**drove [him] out**" (Wallace 526–32; Williams 26). The historical present makes narration in the past vivid and immediate.
- εἰς τὴν ἔρημον is a prepositional phrase (expressing motion toward and into) with εἰς + the accusative, here the acc. sing. fem. of the adjective ἔρημος used as a substantive (object of the preposition) = "**into the desert.**"

<1:13> καὶ ἦν ἐν τῇ ἐρήμῳ τεσσεράκοντα ἡμέρας πειραζόμενος ὑπὸ τοῦ Σατανᾶ, καὶ ἦν μετὰ τῶν θηρίων, καὶ οἱ ἄγγελοι διηκόνουν αὐτῷ. = **And he was in the desert forty days being tested by Satan, and he was with wild animals and the angels were serving him.**

καὶ ἦν ἐν τῇ ἐρήμῳ τεσσεράκοντα ἡμέρας πειραζόμενος ὑπὸ τοῦ Σατανᾶ,

- καί coor. conj. (paratactic/ begins a new sentence) = "**and.**"
- ἦν impf. act. ind. 3rd pers. sing. of the equative verb εἰμί (with the participle constitutes a periphrastic expression) = "**he was [being tested].**"
- ἐν τῇ ἐρήμῳ prepositional phrase (expressing place where) with ἐν + the dative, here the dat. sing. fem. of the adjective ἔρημος (substantive use of the adjective with the article/ object of the preposition/ dative of place where) = "**in the desert**" or "**in the wilderness.**"
- τεσσεράκοντα ἡμέρας acc. plur. fem. of the noun ἡ ἡμέρα, modified by the indeclinable numeral adjective τεσσεράκοντα (accusative of the extent of time) = "**for forty days.**"
- πειραζόμενος pres. pass. participle nom. sing. masc. of the verb πειράζω, agreeing grammatically with the subject of ἦν (a periphrastic use of the participle with the auxilliary verb εἰμί) = "**was being tested**" (Williams 27; contra Decker 15). The periphrastic use of the participle is an elaborate way to express and emphasize what could be expressed with the one-word πειράζω in the imperfect of ongoing action.
- ὑπὸ τοῦ Σατανᾶ, prepositional phrase (expressing agency) with ὑπό + the genitive, here the gen. sing. masc. of the undeclined formal name ὁ Σατανᾶ (object of the preposition/genitive of direct personal agency in conjunction with a verb in the passive voice) = "**by Satan.**" With verbs in the passive voice, impersonal agency is expressed by the dative of means whereas personal agency, as here, is expressed by ὑπό plus the genitive of agency (Smyth 1491–94; Wallace 431–35).

καὶ ἦν μετὰ τῶν θηρίων,

- καὶ coor. conj. (paratactic) = "**and.**"
- ἦν impf. act. ind. 3rd pers. sing. of the equative verb εἰμί (imperfect of an ongoing situation) = "**he (Jesus) was.**"

- μετὰ τῶν θηρίων, prepositional phrase with μετά + the genitive, here the gen. plur. neut. of the noun τὸ θηρίον (object of the preposition/ genitive of association) = "**with the wild animals.**" The article here may serve to make the noun generic = "**with beasts.**" This prepositional phrase may express a friendly and peaceable association but not necessarily so, and the significance of this enigmatic reference to the association of Jesus with the wild animals remains unclear.

καὶ οἱ ἄγγελοι διηκόνουν αὐτῷ.

- καὶ coor. conj. (paratactic) = "**and.**"
- οἱ ἄγγελοι nom. plur. masc. of the noun ὁ ἄγγελος (subject) = "**the angels.**" The article may serve to make this noun generic = "**angels**" or "**messengers.**"
- διηκόνουν impf. act. ind. 3rd pers. plur. of the verb διακονέω (either an imperfect of ongoing action or an inceptive imperfect) = "**[the angels] were serving**" or "**they began serving.**"
- αὐτῷ. dat. sing. masc. of the 3rd pers. personal pronoun αὐτός (the direct object of this verb is in the dative/ dative of association) = "**him.**"

WHAT FOLLOWS

Jesus' baptism and designation as the son or agent of God and his triumph over Satan in the wilderness prepare him and enable him to emerge in Galilee after John's arrest with the announcement that "The rule of God has arrived." Immediately following this proclamation, Jesus' activity of inaugurating the rule of God begins—calling disciples, driving out demons, healing the sick, and so on. The baptism of John, the anointing by the spirit, and the overcoming of temptation have set three key conditions—(1) the preparation of the people, (2) the anointing of the messiah, and (3) the successful overcoming of Satan—whereby the rule of God can begin.

3

The Rule of God and the Call of the Disciples
Mark 1:14–20

PREVIEW

In the few verses of the Gospel that precede this episode, Jesus' identity as "the messiah, the son of God" has been introduced and established. Now, for the first time, he emerges publicly in Galilee where he immediately announces the arrival of God's rulership over the world, a reality made possible in part because Jesus has confronted Satan in the desert and successfully resisted him. The words and actions of Jesus that follow this announcement will display the nature of this rule of God. His first action, the calling of the disciples, demonstrates that God's rule is corporate and that Jesus will share his authority with those who respond to his call to follow him.

⟨1:14⟩ Μετὰ δὲ τὸ <u>παραδοθῆναι</u> τὸν Ἰωάννην
ἦλθεν ὁ Ἰησοῦς εἰς τὴν Γαλιλαίαν
<u>κηρύσσων</u> τὸ <u>εὐαγγέλιον τοῦ θεοῦ</u>
⟨1:15⟩ καὶ λέγων ὅτι
  <u>Πεπλήρωται ὁ καιρὸς</u>
  καὶ <u>ἤγγικεν ἡ βασιλεία τοῦ θεοῦ</u>·

Now after John <u>was handed over</u> (to prison)
Jesus came into Galilee
<u>proclaiming</u> the <u>good news about God</u>
and saying,
  "<u>The time</u> has been <u>fulfilled</u>,
  and <u>the rule of God</u> has <u>arrived</u>.

The Rule of God and the Call of the Disciples

μετανοεῖτε	Repent,
καὶ πιστεύετε ἐν τῷ εὐαγγελίῳ.	and put faith in the good news.
‹1:16› Καὶ παράγων παρὰ τὴν θάλασσαν τῆς Γαλιλαίας	And while passing along by the Sea of Galilee
εἶδεν Σίμωνα	he saw Simon
καὶ Ἀνδρέαν τὸν ἀδελφὸν Σίμωνος	and Andrew the brother of Simon
ἀμφιβάλλοντας ἐν τῇ θαλάσσῃ·	casting (a net) into the sea
ἦσαν γὰρ ἁλιεῖς.	for they were fishermen.
‹1:17› καὶ εἶπεν αὐτοῖς ὁ Ἰησοῦς,	And Jesus said to them,
Δεῦτε ὀπίσω μου,	"Come after me,
καὶ ποιήσω ὑμᾶς γενέσθαι ἁλιεῖς ἀνθρώπων.	and I will make you become fishers of humans.
‹1:18› καὶ εὐθὺς ἀφέντες τὰ δίκτυα	And immediately upon leaving their nets
ἠκολούθησαν αὐτῷ.	they followed him.
‹1:19› Καὶ προβὰς ὀλίγον	And after going ahead a little [further]
εἶδεν Ἰάκωβον τὸν τοῦ Ζεβεδαίου	he saw James the (son of) Zebedee
καὶ Ἰωάννην τὸν ἀδελφὸν αὐτοῦ	and John his brother
καὶ αὐτοὺς ἐν τῷ πλοίῳ	and those in the boat
καταρτίζοντας τὰ δίκτυα,	adjusting their nets
‹1:20› καὶ εὐθὺς ἐκάλεσεν αὐτούς.	And immediately he called them.
καὶ ἀφέντες τὸν πατέρα αὐτῶν Ζεβεδαῖον	And leaving their father Zebedee
ἐν τῷ πλοίῳ μετὰ τῶν μισθωτῶν	in the boat with the hired workers
ἀπῆλθον ὀπίσω αὐτοῦ.	they went off after him.

MARKAN WORD FIELDS

There are two Markan word fields here, one embedded in the other. The first word field is (1) an "apocalyptic announcement," which involves the arrival of "the rule of God" (the activity of God) and "the response of faith" (the correlative human reception of the rule of God). The other word field is (2) the "call and response" of discipleship. This second domain is embedded within the larger context of the apocalyptic arrival of the rule of God and represents an example of it. The narrative frame of these two word fields is an additional word field that represents the beginning of (3) a "journey."

"Apocalyptic Announcement: God's Rule and Human Faith"

The apocalyptic word field is a primary domain of Mark's whole Gospel. Here, the term apocalyptic is used to identify the world shift to God's rulership over the world resulting from Jesus' announcement and the subsequent dénouement laid out in the rest of the narrative leading to the execution.

Jesus has been anointed as the messianic son of God at his baptism by John. After John is arrested, Jesus comes into Galilee and "proclaims" (κηρύσσω) "the good news about God" (τὸ εὐανγγέλιον τοῦ θεοῦ). The announcement that "the time has been fulfilled" (ὁ καιρός πεπλήρωται) marks the temporal beginning of this rulership. The proclamation that "the rule of God has arrived" (ἡ βασιλεία τοῦ θεοῦ ἤγγικεν) signals that God is now acting to take rulership over the world. ἡ βασιλεία is an abstract verbal noun depicting the activity of God in ruling over the world (compare the verb form βασιλεύω). The rest of the narrative of Mark involves the display of this activity of God, who begins to take dominion over the world: the healings, the exorcisms, the works of power over nature, the raising of the dead, the confrontations with authorities, the values Jesus teaches, the commitment to service, the faithfulness of Jesus, the resurrection of Jesus, and the establishment of Jesus at God's right hand. Of course, the call of the disciples belongs to the activity of the rule of God as well. Hence, virtually all word fields in the Gospel are embedded in this encompassing apocalyptic word field.

The correlative commands that follow these two announcements are also part of the apocalyptic domain, because they signal the appropriate human responses to the arrival of God's rule. "Repent" (μετανοεῖτε) and "put faith in the good news" (πιστεύετε τῷ εὐαγγελίῳ) identify how humans are to welcome and respond to God's rule. The "repentance" is the turning from the old way of life, and the "faith" is the embracing of a new way of life as a response to God's rule. Again, the gospel narrative that follows involves a display of the proper responses to God's activity: the repentance of sinners, the faith of suppliants, the actions of those who live the values of God, and the commitment of the disciples to follow Jesus. Of course, there are also the inappropriate or improper human responses to God's rule: resistance by the disciples, a lack of faith among some suppliants, and, mainly, opposition by the authorities. Opposition to God's rule by the authorities is foreshadowed here by the arrest of John the baptizer.

The Rule of God and the Call of the Disciples

Hence, the arrival of God's rule inaugurates a new world, and the narrative that follows displays the divine activity of that rule and the variety of human responses to it.

"Call and Response of Disciples"

Embedded within this new apocalyptic word field is the word field of the "call and response" of the disciples to follow Jesus, who calls disciples and says to Simon and Andrew, "Come after me" (δεῦτε ὀπίσω μου) and adds the promise "I will make you become fishers of people" (ποιήσω ὑμᾶς γενέσθαι ἁλιεῖς ἀνθρώπων). When he saw James and John, immediately "he called them" (ἐκάλεσεν αὐτούς). This is the language of the call of a teacher for disciples, and clearly Jesus is depicted as a teacher. In the very next scene, for example, he enters the synagogue in Capernaum and begins teaching. As we shall see, however, Jesus is not an ordinary teacher. He offers a "new teaching with authority" because he is the agent of the rule of God. In a sense, he is a teacher who is the definitive agent of the rule of God.

In turn, the fishermen respond "immediately" (εὐθύς) with acts of repentance and faith. Simon and Andrew "left their nets" (ἀφέντες τὰ δίκτυα) and "followed him" (ἠκολούθησαν αὐτῷ). Then James and John "left their father Zebedee in the boat with the hired workers" (ἀφέντες τὸν πατέρα αὐτῶν Ζεβεδαῖον ἐν τῷ πλοίῳ μετὰ τῶν μισθωτῶν) and "went off after him" (ἀπῆλθον ὀπίσω αὐτοῦ). These actions of the disciples correlate with the announcement at the beginning of the pericope for people to "repent and put faith in the good news." The leaving of family and labor signals a break with the old world (repentance), and the following of Jesus signals the beginning of their new life as disciples in response to the rule of God (putting faith in the good news).

"Journey"

Finally, the narrative frame for these word fields is a journey: Jesus "came into Galilee" (ἦλθεν ὁ Ἰησοῦς εἰς τὴν Γαλιλαίαν); he was "passing by the sea of Galilee" (παράγων παρὰ τὴν θάλασσαν τῆς Γαλιλαίας); he was "going ahead a little" (προβὰς ὀλίγον); and "they went off after him" (ἀπῆλθον ὀπίσω αὐτοῦ). This journey continues through most of the narrative as Jesus moves in and around Galilee and then makes a pilgrimage to Jerusalem. The journey becomes a metaphor for "the way of the Lord," the way of service and self-giving that Jesus travels as he "goes ahead of his disciples" and the way that Jesus invites his disciples to follow as they "go off after him."

STRUCTURAL PATTERNS

This selection has three parts (Noble 404): (1) Jesus' announcement of the rule of God; (2) the call of Simon and Andrew and (3) the call of James and John. There are parallel structures to the three episodes. Jesus' announcement has two parts: (A) the announcement of the rule of God and (B) the call to repent and have faith. So also, each call story has two parts: (A) Jesus' call to be fishers for people (an action of the rule of God) and (B) the response of those called (a response of faith). In each case, the first part has two features: Jesus announces (a) the time is ripe and (b) the rule of God has come near, and in turn the narrator depicts (a) two situations of people fishing (the time is ripe) and (b) Jesus calls them to be fishers for people (the rule of God has arrived). Also, in each case, the second part has two features to it: Jesus calls for (a) repentance and (b) faith, and in turn the disciples (a) leave their nets and family (repentance) and (b) follow Jesus (put faith in the good news). The parallels are indicated by the letters (A) (a) and (B) (b) that accompany the display of the episode that follows:

Setting:
<1:14> Now after John was handed over (to prison)
    Jesus came into Galilee

Situation:
    proclaiming the good news about God

Reply to the situation:
    <1:15> and saying,
        "The time has been fulfilled,   a   A
    and the rule of God has arrived.   b
        Repent,   a   B
    and put faith in the good news."   b

Setting:
<1:16> And passing along by the Sea of Galilee,

Situation:
    he saw Simon
    and Andrew the brother of Simon   a   A

The Rule of God and the Call of the Disciples

casting (a net) into the sea,
    for they were fishermen.

Reply to the situation:
<1:17> And Jesus said to them,
    "Come after me,   b
    and I will make you become fishers for humans.

Consequence:
<1:18> And immediately leaving the nets   a   B
    they followed him.   b

Setting:
<1:19> And after going ahead a little [further]

Situation:
    he saw James the (son of) Zebedee   a   A
    and John his brother
    and those in the boat
    adjusting the nets

Reply to the situation:
<1:20> And immediately he called them.   b

Consequence:
And leaving their father Zebedee
    in the boat with the hired workers   a   B
they went off after him.   b

This episode occurs within a larger structural pattern in that "the proclamation of the rule of God" and "the calling of disciples" seem to be two events in the first day of Jesus' public activity: (1) he emerges in Galilee to announce the rule of God; (2) goes along the sea of Galilee where he calls two sets of disciples; (3) enters the synagogue at Capernaum where he teaches and drives out a demon; (4) goes to the house of Simon and Andrew where he heals Peter's mother-in-law; and (5) the day concludes after the sun set (actually the beginning of the next day) with the whole city gathered at the door to receive healing and exorcism. The key to this pattern is that Mark wishes to portray it as typical. Early the next morning, Jesus will say to Simon and those with him, "Let's go on to the next towns so I might proclaim there too." And the narrator will add, "And so he went proclaiming in their synagogues throughout Galilee and driving out the demons." The narrative implication is that the day(s) in the next village will replicate the first day and will include proclamation, calling, teaching, exorcism, healing, and large crowds. Then Jesus will move on to repeat this activity in other towns "throughout Galilee."

LITERARY DEVICES

We can place the episode of the call of the disciples (1:16–20) into one of the larger structures of the Gospel, namely Mark's pattern of "episodes in a series of three." The episode of Jesus' calling two sets of disciples is the first in a series of three episodes that together set out the call of the disciples and the fulfillment of the promise of Jesus to make the disciples fishers of people. In this first episode (1:16–20), Jesus calls disciples and promises to make them fishers for people. In the second episode of the series (3:13–19), Jesus goes up on a mountain, summons twelve followers to him, and appoints them to be with him and to drive out demons. In the third episode of the series (6:7–12), Jesus sends out the twelve in pairs to call people to repent, to drive out demons, and to heal. All three episodes are related in a progression, and together they show the full meaning, in Markan terms, of what was meant by the metaphorical expression, "fishers of people."

This series of three is the first in several such series that focus on the disciples. This particular series of three episodes emphasizes the success of the disciples in becoming faithful followers of Jesus. However, most of the other series of three related episodes highlight the failure of the disciples: three boat scenes in which they fail to have faith (4:35–41; 6:47–52; 8:13–21); three bread scenes in which the fail to understand (6:30–44; 8:1–10; 8:13–21); three passion predictions in which they resist Jesus' teaching about his death (8:27–33; 9:30–37; 10:32–45); three times Jesus comes to find them sleeping at Gethsemane (14:32–42), and three times Peter denies Jesus (14:66–72).

LINGUISTIC COMMENTARY

<1:14> Μετὰ δὲ τὸ παραδοθῆναι τὸν Ἰωάννην ἦλθεν ὁ Ἰησοῦς εἰς τὴν Γαλιλαίαν κηρύσσων τὸ εὐαγγέλιον τοῦ θεοῦ = **Now after John was handed over (to prison), Jesus came into Galilee in order to proclaim the good news about God...**

- Μετὰ δὲ τὸ παραδοθῆναι τὸν Ἰωάννην

The Rule of God and the Call of the Disciples

- δὲ postpositive coord. conj. (introducing new information/ beginning a new scene) = "**Now**."
- Μετὰ ... τὸ παραδοθῆναι prepositional phrase with μετά + the infinitive in the accusative, here the acc, sing. neut. article with aor. pass. infinitive of the verb παραδίδωμι (articular infinitive as object of the preposition, the preposition indicating time previous to the time of the main verb) = "**after [John} was arrested**" or (more literally) "**after John's being handed over**." An infinitive is a verbal noun. Here, it is an articular infinitive (takes an article) and, therefore, serves as a substantive. In this case, the articular infinitive is the object of a preposition, μετά, which takes the accusative (hence the acc. sing. neut. article with the indeclinable infinitive παραδοθῆναι) = (literally) "**after the act of being handed over**" or **after being arrested**.

Παραδίδωμι is a key Markan word meaning "handed over" [to prison or judgment] or "arrested" or "bound over." This legal term is connected with arrests and courts, and, in Mark, it expresses the vulnerability to persecution of those agents of the rule of God who proclaim—first John, then Jesus (e. g. 9:30; 10:33), and finally, projected into the future of the story world, the disciples (13:9).

- τὸν Ἰωάννην acc. sing. masc. of the noun ὁ Ἰωάννης = **John**. As a verbal noun, an infinitive (παραδοθῆναι) can take subjects and objects, both of which are expressed in the accusative (and distinguished by word order and context). Here there is only a subject (passive infinitives, like passive verbs, do not take direct objects). Τὸν Ἰωάννην is therefore the subject of the passive action expressed in the infinitive = "**John was handed over**."

There are two ways to translate this construction in English. To retain the nominal (noun) syntax of the articular infinitive, we can translate the construction as a prepositional phrase with the infinitive functioning as a gerund that is the object of the preposition = "**after John's being handed over**." This translation cannot, however, render the voice and tense of the infinitive. To retain these verbal aspects of the infinitive, we can render the construction as a temporal relative clause = "**Now after John was handed over**."

John was handed over into custody at this point. The agent of the passive infinitive (παραδοθῆναι) is unexpressed. Later in Mark, we learn that it was Herod, the [Roman client] king or more accurately the tetrarch in Galilee, who had arrested John, held him in prison, and finally beheaded him (6:17–29). Here, as a foreshadowing, Mark gives readers only a vague, ominous note about John's arrest, whereas later Mark gives us the full story.

ἦλθεν ὁ Ἰησοῦς εἰς τὴν Γαλιλαίαν.

- ὁ Ἰησοῦς nom. sing. masc. of the proper name ὁ Ἰησοῦς (subject) = "**Jesus**." Proper names in Greek, unlike English, often take an article. The presence of the article might denote previous reference (Smyth 1120b) = "**this Jesus, the one referred to above**."

- ἦλθεν 2nd aor. act. ind. 3rd pers. sing. of the deponent verb ἔρχομαι (punctiliar aorist) = "**came**." The word ἔρχομαι is a key verbal thread in Mark and is associated with the purpose and mission of Jesus as agent of the rule of God (e. g. 1:7, 38; 2:17).

- εἰς τὴν Γαλιλαίαν prepositional phrase (expressing motion toward and into) with εἰς + the accusative, here the acc. sing. fem of the noun ἡ Γαλιλαία = "**into Galilee**."

κηρύσσων τὸ εὐαγγέλιον τοῦ θεοῦ.

- κηρύσσων pres. act. participle nom. sing. masc. of the verb κηρύσσω, agreeing with the subject ὁ Ἰησοῦς and therefore describing his action (present circumstantial participle) = "**proclaiming**." This participle could be a temporal circumstantial participle, which in the present tense depicts action contemporaneous with the time of the main verb = "**he came proclaiming**." More likely, it is a circumstantial participle of purpose = "**he came in order to proclaim**." After verbs denoting to come, to go, to send, to summon, and so on, the participle generally denotes purpose (Smyth, 2065).

- τὸ εὐαγγέλιον acc. sing. neut. of the noun τὸ εὐαγγέλιον (direct object of the participle) = [proclaiming] "**the good news**" or "**the gospel**."

- τοῦ θεοῦ gen. sing. masc. of the noun ὁ θεός. There are three choices here for the syntax. (1) The genitive τοῦ θεοῦ is either a genitive of origin (= "**the good news from God**") or, more likely, (2) an objective genitive in which God is the object of the good news (= "**good news about God**"). (3) It is possible, but not likely, that the genitive here serves *both* as a subjective genitive and an objective genitive, making it

The Rule of God and the Call of the Disciples

a "plenary genitive" (Wallace 121) = "**the good news that God brings**" *and* "**the good news about God.**"

<1:15> καὶ λέγων ὅτι Πεπλήρωται ὁ καιρὸς καὶ ἤγγικεν ἡ βασιλεία τοῦ θεοῦ· μετανοεῖτε καὶ πιστεύετε ἐν τῷ εὐαγγελίῳ. = **and [in order] to say, "The time has been fulfilled, and the rule of God has arrived. Repent, and put faith in the good news."**

καὶ λέγων ὅτι

- καί coor. conj. (connects two circumstantial participles, κηρύσσων and λέγων) = "**and.**"
- λέγων pres. act. participle nom. sing. masc. of the verb λέγω, agreeing with ὁ Ἰησοῦς and functioning grammatically just like κηρύσσων = "**saying**" or "**in order to say.**" Like κηρύσσων, λέγων may be either a temporal circumstantial participle or a circumstantial participle of purpose. Note that the act of "saying" is not a separate and different action from the act of "proclaiming." Rather the "saying" along with the direct speech that follows *is* the content of the proclaiming = "**in order to proclaim . . . and, in so doing, to say.**"
- ὅτι subord. conj. (introducing direct speech—called either a recitative ὅτι or a ὅτι of direct speech). As such, it is equivalent to a comma and quotation marks with regard to the speech to follow (Wallace 455) = "**, ...**"

Πεπλήρωται ὁ καιρὸς

- ὁ καιρός nom. sing. masc. of the noun ὁ καιρός (subject) = "**the time**" or **the right time.**" The noun καιρός refers not to calendar or clock time, but to time that is appropriate to certain events = "**appointed time**" or "**opportune moment**" or "**time that has run its course [or reached its completion]**" (Bratcher 37).
- Πεπλήρωται perf. pass. ind. 3rd pers. sing. of the verb πληρόω (the perfect expresses a completed action that has ongoing effects or establishes a state of affairs that continues into the present) = "**has been fulfilled**" or "**is fulfilled.**" The concept of fulfillment may be misleading, as though it referred to the fulfillment of a promise or a prophecy. Here, instead, the idea is that the time is ripe for the arrival of the rule

of God = "**the time is ripe.**" Idiomatically, the phrase may bear the meaning = "**the circumstances are right.**"

The agent of this passive is unspecified. The passive may refer to a process related to time that, as such, does not have an agent. Or the implied agent of the passive could be God, who has now brought the time to fulfillment. A passive in which God is the implied agent is referred to as a "divine passive" (Porter 65).

καὶ ἤγγικεν ἡ βασιλεία τοῦ θεοῦ·

- καί coord. conj. (paratactic, connects this sentence with the previous one) = "**and.**"
- ἡ βασιλεία nom. sing. fem. of the noun ἡ βασιλεία (subject) = "**the [active] rule**" or "**the reign**" or [possibly] "**the kingdom** or **the realm.**" Rather than naming a place, the word βασιλεία depicts activity, with the idea that God is taking active rulership over the world through the words and actions of Jesus, who functions as God's agent. The nominal suffix -εια forms abstract nouns from verbs ending in -ευω, which denote a condition or an activity (Smyth 866.4 and 840, a.9). Hence, the noun βασιλεία is a verbal noun that depicts the activity of reigning (compare the verb form βασιλεύω). Insofar as space is concerned, the term also implies the arena in which such actions occur, as in "has arrived."
- τοῦ θεοῦ gen. sing. masc. of the noun ὁ θεός. The genitive could be a possessive genitive, which would emphasize the spatial dimensions of βασιλεία as a kingdom or a realm (= "**God's kingdom**" or "**God's realm**"). More likely, in relation to what we have just noted above, the genitive is a subjective genitive, identifying the subject agent of the activity of ruling named by the word βασιλεία = "**the ruling activity of God**" or "**the reign of God**" or "**the governing carried out by God.**"
- ἤγγικεν perf. act. ind. 3rd pers. sing. of the verb ἐγγίζω (the perfect expresses a completed action that has ongoing effects or establishes a state of affairs that continues into the present) = "**has arrived**" (emphasizing the present activity of the rule of God as depicted in Mark) or "**has drawn near**" (emphasizing that the rule of God is about to come fully in the very near future). Considering the parallel with the perfect participle πεπλήρωται and its sense of completion, it may

be best to understand the finite verb ἤγγικεν in the perfect as "has arrived."

μετανοεῖτε καὶ πιστεύετε ἐν τῷ εὐαγγελίῳ.

- μετανοεῖτε pres. act. impv. 2nd pers. plur. of the verb μετανοιέω (a command in the present tense may urge ongoing action, but see below) = "**repent**" or "**turn around**." One way to think of the difference between present and aorist imperatives is to consider that the present tense commands ongoing action and the aorist tense commands a single, specific action. However, another way to understand the distinction between present and aorist commands is to identify the difference between a command in an indefinite situation (present) and a command in a specific situation (aorist). To say "love one another" with no particular occasion in mind, one uses the present. To say "love one another" to a specific group of people on a specific occasion, one uses the aorist. The aorist imperative is used elsewhere in the New Testament on a specific occasion with a particular group or crowd (Acts 2:38; 3:19; 8:22; Rev. 2:5, 16; 3:19). Given these considerations, Mark's use of the imperative in the present tense indicates ongoing action. It indicates the lack of a specific occasion and the lack of a particular crowd to which the command is addressed. Thus, Mark's use of the present imperative in this context probably indicates a general call to ongoing repentance for the many crowds that came to John to "prepare the way of the Lord." In this way, the repentance called for reinforces John's call and also specifies the new action ("put faith in the good news") appropriate to the time of the messiah's arrival on the scene.

The concept of repenting involves not a regret or remorse for sin, but a change of understanding that results in a change of life and behavior, a complete turning around from one way of life to another. The verb μετανοέω is a combination of the root νοῦς (= "**mind**") and the prefix μετα- (= "**change**") and bears the meaning of a fundamental "change of mind." Jesus' call to "repent" repeats the proclaiming of John the baptizer, while the call to "put faith in the good news" goes beyond John—because of the arrival of the rule of God. John's message called people to prepare by putting the (sinful) past behind them (turn from), while Jesus' message called also for people to put faith in the new reality now available to create a new future (turn toward).

- καί coor. conj. (connective, connects the two imperatives) = "**and**."
- πιστεύετε = pres. act. impv. 2nd pers. plur. of the verb πιστεύω (a command in the present tense urges ongoing action or, in this case, a command not made to a specific crowd on a specific occasion) = "**trust**" or "**put faith in**" or "**believe**." Probably the word denotes less the idea of "believing" certain truths than the idea "trusting" or "putting faith in" the activity of God, with the notion that belief is implicit in the act of trust.
- ἐν τῷ εὐαγγελίῳ prepositional phrase with ἐν + the dative, here the dat. sing. neut. of the noun τὸ εὐαγγέλιον = "**in the good news**" (that is, the good news about the arrival of the rule of God). It is unusual to have the verb πιστεύω with the preposition ἐν = "**put faith in**" or "**trust into**." Here, in common with Markan usage elsewhere, the preposition ἐν may be equivalent to the preposition εἰς, expressing the idea of movement toward something, i. e. the movement toward putting faith "into" something or someone (Wallace 359; Moule 80). The term may also mean "give fealty to" the kingdom of God.

In Mark, faith obviously includes a belief in the good news that the rule of God has arrived. As the story develops, however, it becomes clear that, in Mark, πιστεύω depicts not so much belief about something (e. g. that Jesus is the Christ) so much as trust in the ruling power of God to act—to heal and to exorcise demons and to do other works that restore life. Hence, faith is the human posture that is open to the active rule of God. As the story of Mark develops, it becomes clear that such faith is a means to have access to the power of God to act in people's lives.

<1:16> Καὶ παράγων παρὰ τὴν θάλασσαν τῆς Γαλιλαίας εἶδεν Σίμωνα καὶ Ἀνδρέαν τὸν ἀδελφὸν Σίμωνος ἀμφιβάλλοντας ἐν τῇ θαλάσσῃ· ἦσαν γὰρ ἁλιεῖς.
= **And passing along by the sea of Galilee, he saw Simon and Andrew the brother of Simon casting [a net] into the sea, for they were fishermen.**

Καὶ παράγων παρὰ τὴν θάλασσαν τῆς Γαλιλαίας.

- καί coor. conj. (paratactic, connects this sentence with the previous one) = "**and**."

The Rule of God and the Call of the Disciples

- παράγων pres. act. participle nom. sing. masc. of the verb παράγω, agreeing with the subject of the main verb εἶδεν (a circumstantial participle of time which, in the present tense, expresses action contemporaneous with the time of the main verb) = **"passing along"** or **"while going along."** However, by translating circumstantial participles as clauses rather than as English participles (-ing), we can retain more of the verbal markers of Greek participles such as tense and voice = **"as he went along"** or **"while he was going along."**

- παρὰ τὴν θάλασσαν prepositional phrase with παρά + the accusative, here acc. sing. fem. of the noun ἡ θάλασσα = **"beside the sea"** or **"by the lake."** Note the repetition of παρά in the prefix of the participle and in the prepositional phrase. The double occurrence of παρα- may be translated by a single word (= **"beside"**) or by a combination of two words (= **"along beside"**) or by a compound word reflecting the repetition (= **"alongside"**) (Porter 167).

Mark uses the word ἡ θάλασσα (sea) rather than the word ἡ λίμνη (lake) to refer to the lake/sea of Galilee. The word ἡ θάλασσα is a significant term for Mark, a term that symbolized the chaos and destruction of water (e.g., the flood). Jesus, however, tames the chaos by stilling the storm (4:35–41) and by walking on the sea (6:45–52). Jesus performs these actions as agent of the activity of God, who also stilled the storm (Ps 107:23–32) and strode across the sea (Job 9:8). Although the Sea of Galilee was a lake in size (12 miles long and 6 miles wide) and contained fresh water, Mark chose to use the term ἡ θάλασσα. Hence, to translate it as "lake" effaces the Markan associations with the concept of "sea."

- τῆς Γαλιλαίας gen. sing. fem. of the noun ἡ Γαλιλαία (partitive genitive with Galilee being the whole territory of which the lake is a part) = **"of Galilee."** Together the phrase provides a proper name for the lake = **"the Sea of Galilee."**

εἶδεν Σίμωνα καὶ Ἀνδρέαν τὸν ἀδελφὸν Σίμωνος.

- εἶδεν 2nd aor. act. ind. 3rd pers. sing. of the verb ὁράω (punctiliar aorist) = **"he (Jesus) saw."**

- Σίμωνα acc. sing. masc. of the proper name ὁ Σίμων (first part of a compound direct object) = **"Simon."**

- καί coor. conj. (connective, connecting the two proper names that comprise the direct object) = "**and**."
- Ἀνδρέαν acc. sing. masc. of the proper name ὁ Ἀνδρέας = "**Andrew**."
- τὸν ἀδελφόν acc. sing. masc. of the noun ὁ ἀδελφός (simple apposition to τὸν Ἀνδρέαν) = "**Andrew, the brother**." Here there is full agreement in case, number, and gender between the head noun (τὸν Ἀνδρέαν) and the noun in apposition (τὸν ἀδελφόν). An agreement in case, however, is the only real determinant for apposition, while number and gender may vary (Smyth 976).
- Σίμωνος gen. sing. masc. of the proper name Σίμων (genitive of relationship) = "**[the brother] of Simon**."

ἀμφιβάλλοντας ἐν τῇ θαλάσσῃ·

- ἀμφιβάλλοντας pres. act. participle acc. plur. masc. of the verb ἀμφιβάλλω (a circumstantial participle of time or a supplementary participle after a verb of perception) = "**casting [nets]**." There are two ways to identify this participle. We may see it as a temporal circumstantial participle which, in the present, expresses action contemporaneous with the time of the main verb. Or we could identify it as a supplementary participle with a verb of physical perception that expresses the action perceived (i. e. Jesus saw "casting"). In both cases, the translation is the same = "**he saw Simon and Andrew ... casting [nets] into the sea**."

The verb ἀμφιβάλλω depicts the throwing out of a circular casting net (BDAG) called an ἀμφίβληστρον. Without a direct object, this word probably refers to a "circular casting-net wound around the arm and thrown out in a rapid circular movement of the arm" (Bratcher 39, quoting Lagrange). The plural number of the accusative ἀμφιβάλλοντας (representing the combination of the two singular direct objects Σίμωνα and Ἀνδρέαν) makes it clear that both brothers were engaged in the act of casting. It is not clear if Mark is depicting both brothers casting one net or each brother casting a net. The plural "nets" in the next verse, however, may imply that the two fishermen are depicted as casting more than one net.

- ἐν τῇ θαλάσσῃ prepositional phrase (expressing place where) with ἐν + the dative, here the dat. sing. fem. of the noun ἡ θάλασσα (dative of place where) = "**in the sea**." In typical Markan fashion, ἐν ("in") may

The Rule of God and the Call of the Disciples

simply equal εἰς = "**into the sea.**" The verb ἀμφιβάλλω takes a prepositional phrase that describes the target of the casting.

ἦσαν γὰρ ἁλιεῖς.

- γάρ postpositive coor. conj. (explanatory conjunction introducing an explanatory clause) = "**for.**"
- ἦσαν impf. ind. 3rd pers. plur. of the equative verb εἰμί (an equative verb depicting an ongoing state or condition) = "**they were.**"
- ἁλιεῖς nom. plur. masc. of the noun ὁ ἁλιεύς (predicate noun, agreeing with the subject of the sentence) = "**fishermen.**" This literal reference to fishermen becomes the basis for its metaphorical use in the next line.

<1:17> καὶ εἶπεν αὐτοῖς ὁ Ἰησοῦς, Δεῦτε ὀπίσω μου, καὶ ποιήσω ὑμᾶς γενέσθαι ἁλιεῖς ἀνθρώπων. = **and Jesus said to them, "Come after me, and I will make you become fishers of humans."**

καὶ εἶπεν αὐτοῖς ὁ Ἰησοῦς,

- καί coor. conj. (paratactic, connecting this sentence with the previous one) = "**and.**"
- εἶπεν 2nd aor. act. ind. 3rd pers. sing. of the verb λέγω (punctiliar aorist) = "**he said.**"
- ὁ Ἰησοῦς nom. sing. masc. of the proper name ὁ Ἰησοῦς (subject) = "**Jesus.**"
- αὐτοῖς dat. plur. masc. of the 3rd pers. personal pronoun (indirect object) = "**to them.**"

Δεῦτε ὀπίσω μου,

- Δεῦτε adverb δεῦρο, (functions like an imperative) = "**Come!**" or "**Come here.**" The imperatival function of an adverb represents an unusual use of an adverb. This unusual use of δεῦτε as a seeming imperative is due to the ellipsis of the imperative ἔλθεσθε (come) in the expression ἔλθεσθε δεῦτε = "**Come here.**" The expression was used so frequently that the imperative could be dropped and the meaning still conveyed by the adverb. Parallels in English would be the use of the adverb "Now!" to convey the imperative phrase "Do it now!" and the use of the adverb "Here!" to convey the imperative phrase "Come here!" Δεῦτε is the adverb used in plural contexts, while δεῦρο is the adverb used in singular contexts and with an elided singular imperative.

- ὀπίσω μου prepositional phrase with ὀπίσω + the genitive, here the gen. sing. of the 1st pers. personal pronoun ἐγώ = "**after me**." Ὀπίσω is a preposition either of time or of place ("after" or "behind"). Here the emphasis is on temporal succession. Jesus comes "after" John (1:7), and the disciples are to come "after" Jesus (8:34). Note also how, for Mark, "coming after" is a correlative to Jesus' "going ahead" (16:7). The whole phrase is equivalent to the command "follow me."

καὶ ποιήσω ὑμᾶς γενέσθαι ἁλιεῖς ἀνθρώπων.

- καί coor. conj. (connecting the two independent clauses of this sentence) = "**and**."
- ποιήσω fut. act. ind. 1st pers. sing. of the verb ποιέω (promissory future or intentional future expressing a commitment of the speaker to do something) = "**I will make**."
- ὑμᾶς acc. plur. of the 2nd pers. personal pronoun σύ = "**you**." Ordinarily, this would be the first of two accusatives that usually come after verbs of making, naming, appointing, and so on = "make you fishers." The sentence, however, has an object clause expressed by an infinitive. As such, the accusative ὑμᾶς is the direct object of ποιήσω and it is also the subject of the infinitive γενέσθαι. In other sentences where the subject of the infinitive is the same as the direct object of the governing verb, that subject is not repeated in connection with the infinitive (Smyth 1972).
- ἁλιεῖς acc. plur. masc. of the noun ὁ ἁλιεύς) = "**fishers**." Ordinarily, this second accusative would serve as the second object of ποιέω, as a verb that takes two accusatives. The whole clause would be, "I will make you fishers." However, because the infinitive of the object clause (γενέσθαι) is present, ἁλιεῖς functions as the predicate noun of that infinitive. Usually, a predicate noun following a linking verb (such as γενέσθαι) is in the nominative, not the accusative. However, ἁλιεῖς here stands in the accusative, because the predicate noun of an equative

verb stands in the same case as the subject of the linking verb, which in this case is the accusative pronoun ὑμᾶς.

- γενέσθαι aor. mid. (in form) inf. of the deponent equative verb γίνομαι (object infinitive—Smyth 1991, 1994) = "**to become.**" Because an infinitive is a verbal noun, it can take a subject and a direct object (or a predicate noun). Because γενέσθαι is an equative verb, it takes a predicate noun rather than a direct object. Here, the subject of the infinitive is ὑμᾶς and the predicate noun after the infinitive (γενέσθαι, which, as we have said, is an equative verb) is ἁλιεῖς (Wallace 195). Hence, the translation is "**I will make you (to) become fishers of humans.**"

The subject and predicate noun of an equative verb are always in the same case. Usually, they are in the nominative case, even when it is an infinitive. They are both nominative when the subject of the infinitive of the linking verb is the same as the subject of the governing verb. However, when the subject of the infinitive (γενέσθαι) is different from the subject of the governing verb (ποιήσω), then the subject and predicate noun are in the accusative. Because the subject of an infinitive and the predicate noun (or object) of an infinitive are in the same case, they are usually (as here) distinguished by word order (the subject coming first).

The use of γίνομαι ("become") rather than εἰμί ("be") may refer to the future "process" by which the disciples become fishers for people, as depicted over the series of the three call episodes (see above under "structure").

- ἀνθρώπων gen. plur. masc. of the noun ὁ ἄνθρωπος (an objective genitive, with "people" being the object of the action of fishing depicted by the agent noun "fishers" [compare the verb ἁλιεύω]—Smyth 843 a. 1) = "**fishers of humans**" or "**fishers for humans.**" This metaphorical use of "fishers" is the first instance of Jesus' use of metaphorical language. Such metaphorical language in Mark's narrative manifests itself primarily in Jesus' allegorical parables.

This call to discipleship is an expression of the good news of the rule of God in as much as it invites people into a purpose commensurate with divine activity. Jeremiah 16:16 foretells that God will use fishermen to gather the dispersed and exiled people of God. Similarly, Jesus calls fishers to be agents in proclaiming the rule of God.

<1:18> καὶ εὐθὺς ἀφέντες τὰ δίκτυα ἠκολούθησαν αὐτῷ. = **And immediately leaving their nets, they followed him.**

καὶ εὐθὺς ἀφέντες τὰ δίκτυα

- καί coor. conj. (paratactic, connects this sentence to the previous one) = "**and**."
- εὐθύς adverb (temporal) = "**immediately**" or "**at once**." Εὐθύς is a common Markan adverb that conveys here the readiness of the disciples to respond quickly and without hesitation to Jesus' invitation.
- ἀφέντες aor. act. participle nom. plur. masc. of the verb ἀφίημι, agreeing with the subject of the main verb "they," that is, Simon and Andrew (circumstantial participle which, in the aorist, expresses action previous to the time of the main verb) = "**after leaving [the nets]**" or (simply) "**leaving**" or "**when they had left [the nets]**." "Leaving the nets" parallels Jesus' command to "Repent" (turn from), while "Follow me" parallels the command to "Put faith in the good news" (turn toward).
- τὰ δίκτυα acc. plur. neut. of the noun τὸ δίκτυον (direct object of the participle) = "**their nets**." Note this is the generic term for nets. As suggested by the context, the definite article here takes the place of an unemphatic possessive pronoun (Smyth 1120) = "**their [nets]**."

There are two possible explanations implied by the text as to why the disciples leave their nets "immediately" to follow Jesus. One is that they have heard the announcement about the rule of God that Jesus was proclaiming in Galilee. The other is that they were responding to the potential elevation in honor that would come with becoming disciples of a teacher. In either case, the story implies that their response was an expression of the invitation to "put faith in the good news." Of course, their immediate response also serves the narrative purpose of reflecting favorably on the authority of Jesus as one who will speak and get results. We learn later in Mark's narrative that the disciples do not have the same idea that Jesus has about what it means to follow him.

ἠκολούθησαν αὐτῷ.

- ἠκολούθησαν aor. act. ind. 3rd pers. plur. of the verb ἀκολουθέω (punctiliar aorist or inceptive aorist) = "**they followed him**." The aorist ἠκολούθησαν could depict the single action of following Jesus (punctiliar). Or it could express the beginning of an action that will continue (inceptive) = "**they began to follow**." This is a key term in Mark that is used of the twelve and others to express discipleship (compare, for example, 2:14; 8:34; 10:21; 15:40–41).

- αὐτῷ dat. sing. masc. of the 3rd pers. personal pronoun αὐτός (dative of complement/ direct object in the dative after verbs of "following") = **"him (Jesus)."** When the dative functions as a direct object, it may be preferable to refer to it as a "complementary dative" to distinguish the different semantics of the dative and accusative cases (Smyth 1460). Wallace notes "that such datives are usually related to verbs implying personal relation" (171). Thus, this dative highlights the personal relationship between these disciples and Jesus.

<1:19> Καὶ προβὰς ὀλίγον εἶδεν Ἰάκωβον τὸν τοῦ Ζεβεδαίου καὶ Ἰωάννην τὸν ἀδελφὸν αὐτοῦ καὶ αὐτοὺς ἐν τῷ πλοίῳ καταρτίζοντας τὰ δίκτυα, = **And going ahead a little, he saw James the son of Zebedee and John his brother and those in the boat adjusting their nets.**

Καὶ προβὰς ὀλίγον

- καί coor. conj. (paratactic, connecting this sentence with the previous one) = **"and."**
- προβάς aor. act. participle nom. sing. masc. of the verb προβαίνω agreeing with the subject "he" (Jesus) of the main verb of the sentence (temporal circumstantial participle which, in the aorist, expresses time previous to the time of the main verb) = **"after going ahead"** or **"after he proceeded."**
- ὀλίγον acc. sing. neut. of the adjective ὀλίγος, η, ον which serves as an adverb (adverbial accusative of "place where") = **"a little (further)."** Adjectives standing alone in the accusative singular neuter often function as adverbs.

εἶδεν Ἰάκωβον τὸν τοῦ Ζεβεδαίου καὶ Ἰωάννην τὸν ἀδελφὸν αὐτοῦ

- εἶδεν aor. act. ind. 3rd pers. sing. of the verb ὁράω (punctiliar aorist) = **"he saw."**
- Ἰάκωβον acc. sing. masc. of the proper name ὁ Ἰάκωβος (first part of a compound direct object) = **"James"** (Jacob!).
- τόν acc. sing. masc. of the definite article ὁ (an article by itself functioning as a substantive and standing for τὸ υἱόν) = **"the [son]."** The

article is in simple apposition to Ἰάκωβον, a noun following another noun in the same case [and usually also agreeing in number and gender] and expressing the same thing in other words, here τὸν υἱόν ("the son"), with the υἱόν being elided.

The construction may be explained in a way different from the assumption that the substantive υἱόν has been elided. Smyth (1142a) states that the genitive following a proper name is sufficient in itself to express sonship (without assuming an ellipsis) and is the structure of official designation that merely states the parentage of the person. When the definite article takes the same case as the proper name and precedes the genitive, the article serves to distinguish this person from other people with the same name. Therefore, here in Mark, the addition of the definite article τόν after the proper name James may indicate that there are others in the same extended family or village with the same name (see Mark 6:3) = "**Zebedee's James.**"

- τοῦ Ζεβεδαίου gen. sing. masc. of a proper name (genitive of relationship) = "**of Zebedee**" or "**Zebedee's James.**"
- καί coor. conj. (simple connective, connects the two proper names of this compound direct object of the verb εἶδεν) = "**and.**"
- Ἰωάννην acc. sing. masc. of the proper name Ἰωάννης (second part of a compound direct object) = "**John.**" After a καί connective, the sentence adds another direct object of the verb, thereby forming a compound direct object.
- τὸν ἀδελφόν acc. sing. masc. of the noun ὁ ἀδελφός (simple apposition in the accusative, agreeing with Ἰωάννην as a noun following another noun and referring to the same person or thing) = "**the brother.**"
- αὐτοῦ gen. sing. masc. of the 3rd pers. personal pronoun αὐτός (genitive of relationship) = "**[the brother] of him (i. e. James)**" or "**his (i. e. James') [brother].**"

καὶ αὐτοὺς ἐν τῷ πλοίῳ

- καί coor. conj. (simple connective, connects the pronoun αὐτούς to the previous two proper names of this compound direct object) = "**and.**" With this καί connective, the sentence adds a third part to this compound direct object of the verb.

- αὐτούς acc. plur. masc. of the 3rd pers. personal pronoun = "**them**" or, as a substitute for a demonstrative pronoun = "**those**" or simply "**the others.**" This could be a reference to the "hired workers" whom James and John subsequently left in the boat with their father Zebedee. Less likely is the suggestion that αὐτούς is a repetition of the two brothers, i. e. "He saw James and John and [he saw] them in the boat. . . ." (Zerwick #377). Understood this way, the phrase could be made subordinate in translation, as in "who were in the boat" or "while they were in the boat" (Bratcher 42). However, this explanation confuses the Greek grammar.

- ἐν τῷ πλοίῳ prepositional phrase (expressing place where) with ἐν + the dative, here dat. sing. neut. of the noun τὸ πλοῖον (dative of place where) = "**in the boat.**" The article can sometimes function as a possessive and may here mean "in their boat."

καταρτίζοντας τὰ δίκτυα,

- καταρτίζοντας pres. act. participle acc. plur. masc. of the verb καταρτίζω agreeing with the accusatives of the direct objects and relating grammatically/inclusively to all of them—James, John, and others (a circumstantial participle of time or a supplementary participle after a verb of perception) = "**adjusting [the nets].**" There are two ways to identify this participle. We may see it as a temporal circumstantial participle which, in the present, expresses action contemporaneous with the time of the main verb = "**while mending.**" Or we could identify it as a supplementary participle with a verb of physical perception that expresses the action perceived (i. e. Jesus saw "adjusting"). Literally, the word means "to render complete" and therefore "to repair."

- τὰ δίκτυα acc. plur. neut. of the noun τὸ δίκτυον (direct object of the participle) = "**the nets.**" As suggested by the context, the definite article here takes the place of an unemphatic possessive pronoun (Smyth 1120) = "**their [nets].**" Mark employs the word "nets" in both episodes as a symbol for the idea that the disciples were leaving behind their source of livelihood and security to follow Jesus.

<1:20> καὶ εὐθὺς ἐκάλεσεν αὐτούς. καὶ ἀφέντες τὸν πατέρα αὐτῶν Ζεβεδαῖον ἐν τῷ πλοίῳ μετὰ τῶν μισθωτῶν ἀπῆλθον ὀπίσω αὐτοῦ. = **And immediately**

he called them. And leaving their father Zebedee in the boat with the hired workers, they went off after him.

καὶ εὐθὺς ἐκάλεσεν αὐτούς.

- καί coor. conj. (paratactic, connecting this sentence to the previous sentence) = "**and**."
- εὐθύς adverb (temporal, emphasizing the urgency of Jesus' invitation offered without hesitation = "**immediately**" or "**at once**."
- ἐκάλεσεν aor. act. ind. 3rd pers. sing. of the verb καλέω (punctiliar aorist) = "**he (Jesus) called**." In this contract verb, unlike most epsilon contract verbs, the epsilon does not lengthen to an eta before the sigma infix of the aorist tense (Smyth 4886).
- αὐτούς acc. plur. masc. of 3rd pers. personal pronoun αὐτός, ή, ό (direct object) = "**them**" (probably refers only to James and John, because of the reference in the following clause to "*their* father"). Καλέω is a key Markan term depicting Jesus' invitation to the discipleship of following him.

καὶ ἀφέντες τὸν πατέρα αὐτῶν Ζεβεδαῖον

- Καί coor. conj. (paratactic, connecting this sentence to the previous one) = "**and**."
- ἀφέντες aor. act. participle nom. plur. masc. of the verb ἀφίημι, agreeing with the yet-to-be-mentioned subject of the main verb ("they" = James and John) (temporal circumstantial participle which, in the aorist, expresses time previous to the time of the main verb) = "**after leaving**" or simply "**leaving**" or "**after they left**" or "**they left [their father Zebedee and**."
- τὸν πατέρα acc. sing. masc. of the noun ὁ πατήρ (direct object of the participle) = "**the father**."
- αὐτῶν gen. plur. masc. of the 3rd pers. personal pronoun αὐτός, -ή, -ό (genitive of relationship) = "**[the father] of them**" or "**their [father]**." The antecedent to the pronoun is James and John.
- Ζεβεδαῖον acc. sing. masc. of the proper name ὁ Ζεβεδαῖος, agreeing with τὸν πατέρα (simple apposition in the accusative to τὸν πατέρα) = "**Zebedee**" as in "their father, Zebedee."

The Rule of God and the Call of the Disciples

ἐν τῷ πλοίῳ μετὰ τῶν μισθωτῶν

- ἐν τῷ πλοίῳ prepositional phrase (expressing place where) with ἐν + the dative, here dat. sing. neut. of the noun τὸ πλοῖον (object of the preposition/ dative of place where) = **"in the boat."**
- μετὰ τῶν μισθωτῶν prepositional phrase (expressing association) with μετά + the genitive, here gen. plur. masc. of the noun ὁ μισθωτός = **"with the hired workers."** Μισθωτός literally means "paid person," derived from ὁ μισθός, which means "pay" or "wages." Hence, τῶν μισθωτῶν refers to day laborers, not slaves or members of the family, but people without permanent work. Most likely, the "hired workers" identify the "others in the boat," referenced in the previous verse. The workers would have been connected more to Zebedee than to his sons, because it is likely that the father would have been the head of this fishing collective.

ἀπῆλθον ὀπίσω αὐτοῦ.

- ἀπῆλθον 2nd aor. act. ind. 3rd person plur. of the deponent verb ἀπέρχομαι (punctiliar aorist) = **"they went off"** or **"they went away"** or **"they departed."**
- ὀπίσω αὐτοῦ prepositional phrase (expressing association) with ὀπίσω + the genitive, here the gen. sing. masc. of the 3rd pers. personal pronoun αὐτός, ἡ, ὁ (object of the preposition/ genitive of association) = **"after him."** (Jesus). The common adverb ὀπίσω is used here as a preposition of time or place that takes the genitive. The whole phrase parallels the initial call of Jesus to Simon and Andrew and forms an inclusio to the whole episode: Jesus says to Simon and Andrew, δεῦτε ὀπίσω μου ("Come *after me*"), and later the narrator says of James and John ἀπῆλθον ὀπίσω αὐτοῦ ("They went off *after him*").

These two stories of the calling of disciples parallel each other in structure and content—with the repetition of words (verbal threads), grammatical forms, syntactical structures, and word order. Together they reinforce the call to discipleship, the importance of an immediate response, and the radical nature of the break from family and work that is involved in following Jesus. Note also that Jesus does not call those he heals to discipleship. Rather, he tells them to "go off" or "go to your house" or to "be quiet." This approach undercuts the typical patron-client transactions where the client is expected to respond to a favor by following or touting the patron—in favor of a freely given action.

What follows. After these two scenes depicting the call and response of disciples, the narrator leads the readers through a series of episodes in which the disciples play only minor and secondary roles, while Jesus drives out demons, heals the sick, and engages in public conflicts with the authorities—all displays of the arrival of the rule of God. By means of brief references and minor involvements, however, the narrator does not let the reader forget that the disciples are present in these episodes. Nevertheless, the disciples do not play a prominent role again until the second episode in the "series of three" call episodes, when Jesus takes twelve aside privately on a mountain and appoints them as people who will be with him and who will have authority to drive out demons (3:13–19).

4

Jesus the Exorcist
Mark 1:21–28

PREVIEW

This is the first public action of Jesus as exorcist and (in the episode that follows) healer. After Jesus calls four fishermen to follow him, they enter the synagogue at Capernaum on the Sabbath where Jesus teaches and then exorcizes an unclean spirit. Perhaps it is appropriate, after his recent confrontation with Satan, that Jesus should show his conquest over Satan by exorcizing a demon. The connection between this episode and the earlier testing by Satan is confirmed by the fact that the unclean spirit in Capernaum, as a minion of Satan, knows who Jesus is and believes he has come to destroy them (demons). Jesus' teaching and exorcism elicit amazement from those present, whereupon the crowds connect the exorcism to the teaching and ask, "What is this? A new teaching with authority?

| ‹1:21› Καὶ εἰσπορεύονται εἰς Καφαρναούμ· καὶ εὐθὺς τοῖς σάββασιν εἰσελθὼν εἰς τὴν συναγωγὴν ἐδίδασκεν. | And they enter into Capernaum and immediately on the Sabbath upon entering into the synagogue, he began teaching. |
| ‹1:22› καὶ ἐξεπλήσσοντο ἐπὶ τῇ διδαχῇ αὐτοῦ· | And they were astonished at his teaching |

ἦν γὰρ <u>διδάσκων</u> αὐτοὺς	for he was <u>teaching</u> them
ὡς <u>ἐξουσίαν</u> ἔχων	as one having <u>authority</u>
καὶ οὐχ ὡς οἱ γραμματεῖς.	and not as the scribes [taught].
‹1:23› καὶ εὐθὺς ἦν	And immediately there was
ἐν τῇ συναγωγῇ αὐτῶν	in their synagogue
ἄνθρωπος ἐν <u>πνεύματι ἀκαθάρτῳ</u>	a man with an <u>unclean spirit</u>.
καὶ ἀνέκραξεν	And he cried out
‹1:24› λέγων,	saying,
Τί <u>ἡμῖν</u> καὶ σοί,	"What [do you have] <u>against us</u>,
Ἰησοῦ Ναζαρηνέ;	Jesus Nazarene?
ἦλθες <u>ἀπολέσαι</u> ἡμᾶς;	Did you come to <u>destroy</u> us?
οἶδά σε τίς εἶ,	I know you, who you are,
<u>ὁ ἅγιος</u> τοῦ θεοῦ.	the <u>holy one</u> of God."
‹1:25› καὶ <u>ἐπετίμησεν</u> αὐτῷ ὁ Ἰησοῦς	And Jesus <u>rebuked</u> it
λέγων,	saying,
Φιμώθητι καὶ ἔξελθε ἐξ αὐτοῦ.	"Be muzzled, and come out of him!"
‹1:26› καὶ σπαράξαν αὐτὸν	And the <u>unclean spirit</u>,
<u>τὸ πνεῦμα τὸ ἀκάθαρτον</u>	convulsing him
καὶ φωνῆσαν φωνῇ μεγάλῃ	and crying in a loud cry,
<u>ἐξῆλθεν</u> ἐξ αὐτοῦ.	<u>came out</u> of him.
‹1:27› καὶ <u>ἐθαμβήθησαν</u> ἅπαντες	And they all together were <u>amazed</u>,
ὥστε συζητεῖν πρὸς ἑαυτοὺς	so that they questioned among themselves
λέγοντας,	saying,
Τί ἐστιν τοῦτο;	"What is this,
<u>διδαχὴ καινὴ</u> κατ' <u>ἐξουσίαν</u>·	a <u>new teaching</u> with <u>authority</u>?
καὶ <u>τοῖς πνεύμασιν τοῖς ἀκαθάρτοις</u>	He <u>commands</u>
<u>ἐπιτάσσει</u>,	even the <u>unclean spirits</u>
καὶ <u>ὑπακούουσιν</u> αὐτῷ.	and they <u>obey</u> him!"
‹1:28› καὶ ἐξῆλθεν	and (there) went out
ἡ ἀκοὴ αὐτοῦ εὐθὺς	the report about him immediately
πανταχοῦ	everywhere,
εἰς ὅλην τὴν περίχωρον τῆς Γαλιλαίας.	into the whole surrounding countryside of Galilee.

MARKAN WORD FIELDS

There are two primary word fields expressed here. The central one is the language domain of (1) "demonic possession and exorcism." At the same time, this central domain is framed by and interpreted in the context of the domain of (2) "teaching with authority." Two further motifs running through the exorcism narrative are (3) "purity and defilement" and (4) "secrecy." The whole episode occurs as part of Jesus' (5) "journey" around Galilee proclaiming the good news. Two minor word fields that provide the setting for this episode are the (6) "Sabbath" and "synagogue." All of it is encompassed within the "rule of God."

"Demonic Possession and Exorcism"

The language of this story focuses on the exorcism Jesus performs. There is a man "with an unclean spirit" (ἐν πνεύματι ἀκαθάρτῳ), and Jesus "rebuked it" (ἐπετίμησεν αὐτῷ). The vehement conflict between Jesus and the demon is expressed in the language of demonic challenge. In two hostile questions, the spirit expresses his terror that Jesus is "against us" (Τί ἡμῖν καὶ σοί) and has "come to destroy us" (ἦλθες ἀπολέσαι ἡμᾶς). It utters the name "Jesus Nazarene" (Ἰησοῦ Ναζαρηνέ) and an epithet "the holy one of God" (ὁ ἅγιος τοῦ θεοῦ) as means to get power over him. Jesus in turn "commands" (ἐπιτάσσει) the unclean spirit to "Be muzzled and come out of him" (Φιμώθητι καὶ ἔξελθε ἐξ αὐτοῦ). And the unclean spirit "obeyed" him (ὑπακούουσιν αὐτῷ). After "shaking" the man (σπαράξαν αὐτὸν) and "screaming in a loud cry" (φωνῆσαν φωνῇ μεγάλῃ), it "came out" of him (ἐξῆλθεν ἐξ αὐτου).

"Teaching with Authority"

The second word field frames this central one and gives a larger context to it. At the beginning of the episode, the people in the synagogue "were astonished at his teaching (ἐξεπλήσσοντο ἐπὶ τῇ διδαχῇ αὐτοῦ·) because he was teaching them "as one having authority" (ὡς ἐξουσίαν ἔχων), and "not like the scribes" (καὶ οὐχ ὡς οἱ γραμματεῖς). Then, at the end, the people in the synagogue again "were all amazed" (ἐθαμβήθησαν ἅπαντες), asking if this was a "new teaching with authority" (διδαχὴ καινὴ κατ' ἐξουσίαν). The episode progresses in its portrayal of Jesus' teaching. It begins with traditional teaching and moves to an action so as to combine the action as part of the teaching. As such, the exorcism is presented as an expression of Jesus' teaching. The depiction of Jesus' "commanding" (ἐπιτάσσει) the unclean spirits and of their "obeying" (ὑπακούουσιν) him belongs, therefore, not only to the exorcism word field but also to the word field of "teaching with authority." To this language field also belong the "astonishment" (ἐξεπλήσσοντο) and the "amazement" (ἐθαμβήθησαν) of the crowd as a public witness to the authority of his teaching as an exorcist. Considering the exorcism, then, the episode progresses from "teaching with authority" (ἐξουσίαν ἔχων) to a "new teaching with authority" (διδαχὴ καινὴ κατ' ἐξουσίαν).

As the story of the Gospel develops, Mark clarifies the nature of Jesus' authority from God. The readers come to learn that Jesus' authority is expressed in service (exorcism, for one) and that this authority does not bow to public pressure. By contrast, the scribes and other leaders have an authority that lords over others, and their authority is based on the approval and domination of other people.

"Purity and Defilement"

Note how the threads of other Markan word fields are running through this episode as minor motifs. The first is the motif of "purity and defilement." The demon is depicted as an "unclean" spirit (πνεύματι ἀκαθάρτῳ), that is, a spirit capable of defiling those who have contact with the possessed person. As a contrast, Jesus is portrayed as the "holy one" of God (ὁ ἅγιος τοῦ θεοῦ), that is, one who is capable of overcoming uncleanness by the power of the "holy" spirit (πνεύματι ἁγίῳ—1:8).

"Secrecy"

The second motif is "secrecy." In Mark, this refers to the so-called messianic secret motif. The demon knows who Jesus is (οἶδά σε τίς εἶ) and threatens to expose Jesus publicly as "the holy one of God" (ὁ ἅγιος τοῦ θεοῦ). Jesus, in turn, orders the demon to "be muzzled" (Φιμώθητι) and to "get out of him" (ἔξελθε ἐξ αὐτοῦ), perhaps, in part, so the spirit could no longer speak. Note in the next episode how Jesus "would not let the demons talk" because "they knew him" (1:34).

"Journey"

All geographical word fields are, in some sense, a part of the word field of the larger Markan motif of the "journey." Jesus and the disciples entered Capernaum (εἰσπορεύονται εἰς Καφαρναούμ) on the sea of Galilee. This is the first village Jesus enters after calling disciples, and, in Mark, he seems to make this his new home (cf. 2:1). However, he does not stay there for long, because early the next morning he moves on. At the end of this episode, the word about Jesus goes out "everywhere into the whole surrounding countryside of Galilee" (πανταχοῦ εἰς ὅλην τὴν περίχωρον τῆς Γαλιλαίας). This news throughout Galilee prepares the way for Jesus to go there. In the next episode, when Jesus' disciples want him to remain in Capernaum due to his popularity, Jesus indeed tells the disciples, "Let's go on to the next towns, so I might proclaim there too" (1:38).

"Sabbath" and "Synagogue"

Finally, a pair of minor motifs running through the early part of Mark are the settings of Sabbath and synagogue. In this episode, the Sabbath (τοῖς σάββασιν) gave Jesus the occasion to teach publicly, and the synagogue (εἰς τὴν συναγωγὴν) provided the audience for his teaching. Eventually, Jesus will withdraw from teaching in the synagogues because of the opposition there. He will turn to houses, open spaces between villages, and the seaside as places of teaching the large crowds who gather to hear him.

"The Rule of God"

Finally, by implication, all these word fields are embedded in the larger display of the arrival of God's rule over all creation. Jesus, the agent of God, has authority over demons. Later in Mark, Jesus will clarify his exorcisms in relation to the rule of God by saying that he has bound (in the testing in the desert) the strong one (Satan) and is now plundering (driving out) his goods (demons) (3:22–30). For other Markan passages related to exorcism, see 3:13–19, 22–30; 5:1–20; 6:7–13; 7:24–30; 9:14–29).

STRUCTURE

The structure of the narrative sequence is rather clear: setting, situation, presentation of the problem, Jesus addressing the problem, the response of the demon, and the consequent reaction of the crowd (Noble 271–272). At the same time, the overall structure seems to reflect the Markan sandwiching technique in which one central episode (the exorcism) is sandwiched between the beginning and ending of another episode. This framing episode (teaching with authority) begins before the central episode and ends after it. The two related stories are experienced temporally by a listening audience such that hearers are held in some suspense, because they have to hear the core story before they can hear the outcome of the framing episode. The two episodes of Markan sandwiches are always connected thematically, as here, although it is unusual for the two episodes to be so intertwined with the same audience in the narrative and to have an outcome for the framing episode that depends on the presence of the core episode.

Note the ABAB pattern. For example, consider the overall sequence of actions, first the teaching (A—1:21-22) and then the exorcism (B—1:23-26). These two actions parallel the words of the crowd at the end of the episode (1:27): first, they comment on the teaching (A—"What is this? A new teaching with authority"), and then they comment on the exorcism (B—"He gives orders even to the unclean spirits and they obey him"). This response by the crowd ties the two actions together so that the exorcism is seen as an expression of Jesus' teaching with authority.

Note also how the three parts of the command of Jesus (a—Jesus "rebuked it" and b—he said, "be muzzled" and c—"come out of him") parallel the results of the command (a—the demon "convulsed the man" and b—"He cried in a loud voice" and c—"it came out of him"). This parallelism emphasizes the authority of Jesus' teaching: he commands, and immediately the demon obeys.

Setting:
<1:21> And they enter into Capernaum

Situation:
and immediately on the Sabbath
    entering into the synagogue,
    he began teaching.   A
<1:22> And they were astonished at his teaching,
    for he was teaching them as one having authority
    and not as the scribes.

Problem:
<1:23> And immediately there was in their synagogue
    a man with an unclean spirit.
And he cried out <1:24>
    saying,
        "What do you have against us,
            Jesus Nazarene?
        Did you come to destroy us?
        I know who you are,
            the holy one of God."

Reply to the problem:
<1:25> And Jesus rebuked it   a   B
    saying,
        "Be muzzled,   b
    and come out of him!"   c

Response:
<1:26> And the unclean spirit, convulsing him   a
and crying in a loud cry,   b
    came out of him.   c

Consequence:
<1:27> And all were amazed,
    so that they were arguing with each other
        saying,
            "What is this?   A
    A new teaching with authority?
        He commands even the unclean spirits   B
    and they obey him!"
<1:28> And (there) went out the report about him immediately
    everywhere,
    into the whole surrounding countryside of Galilee.

This episode occurs within a larger narrative pattern of the first day of Jesus' public activity (1:14–34): (1) Jesus announces the rule of God; (2) calls four disciples; (3) teaches in a synagogue and drives out a demon; (4) heals Peter's mother-in-law; and (5) attends to the crowd that gathers for healing and exorcism. The key to this pattern is that Mark wishes to portray it as typical. Early on the next morning, Jesus will say to Simon and those with him, "Let's go on to the next towns so I might proclaim there too." And the narrator will add, "And so he went proclaiming in their synagogues throughout all Galilee and driving out the demons." The narrative implication is that the day(s) in the next village will resemble this first day (Williams 34). The fact that exorcism is highlighted ("driving out the demons") shows the formative importance of this narrative episode, and it shows the importance of exorcisms in general for Mark's story.

LINGUISTIC COMMENTARY

<1:21> Καὶ εἰσπορεύονται εἰς Καφαρναούμ· καὶ εὐθὺς τοῖς σάββασιν εἰσελθὼν εἰς τὴν συναγωγὴν ἐδίδασκεν. = **And they enter into Capernaum, and immediately on the Sabbath upon entering into the synagogue he began teaching.**

Καὶ εἰσπορεύονται εἰς Καφαρναούμ·

- Καί coord. conj. (paratactic, connects this sentence with the previous sentence) = "**and**."

- εἰσπορεύονται pres. mid. ind. 3rd pers. plur. of the verb εἰσέρχομαι (historical present) = "**they**" (Jesus and those he has called) "**they go into**" or "**they entered into**." In Mark, a historical present may signify a change of setting. On the designation of this verb as a deponent, see the commentary on Mark 1:5.

- εἰς Καφαρναούμ prepositional phrase (expressing movement toward and into) with εἰς + the accusative, here of the indeclinable proper noun ἡ Καφαρναούμ = "**into Capernaum**." Note the repetition of εἰς in the prefix to the verb and as the preposition (Williams 34; Decker 23). This repetition of εἰς may be accounted for by translating them as "entered into Capernaum" (rather than just "entered Capernaum"). Capernaum was a fishing village on the northwestern shore of the Sea of Galilee.

καὶ εὐθὺς τοῖς σάββασιν εἰσελθὼν εἰς τὴν συναγωγὴν ἐδίδασκεν

- καί coor. conj. (paratactic, connects this sentence with the previous one) = "**and**."

- εὐθὺς adverb (temporal) = "**immediately.**" Here εὐθύς reinforces the purposefulness and urgency of Jesus' activity = "**as soon as [it was the Sabbath].**"
- τοῖς σάββασιν dat. plur. neut. of the noun τὸ σάββατον (dative of time when) = "**on the Sabbath.**" The dative plural of the second declension noun σάββατον should be σαββάτοις. Frequently, however, the noun takes the third declension neuter plural ending -σι as though from the noun σάββας. The plural is idiomatic and probably refers here to a single Sabbath. Sabbath was the day of rest, beginning on Friday after sunset when the first three night lights appeared and ending on Saturday (Sabbath) the same time of day. The Sabbath day, set aside for rest, nevertheless included going to the village synagogue to worship and learn. On the first Sabbath after Jesus entered Capernaum, he entered the synagogue.

We might take τοῖς σάββασιν as a plural designating many Sabbaths. This translation might make sense in light of the imperfect verb ἐδίδασκεν, which would then be taken as an iterative imperfect (rather than an inceptive imperfect). In such a case, the translation would be "and immediately on the sabbaths he would customarily enter into the synagogue and teach." This translation is rendered less probable by the fact that the whole episode makes it clear that Mark is narrating an event that takes place on one specific Sabbath day.

Sunset marked the beginning and ending of every day. Actually, the evening watch began at sunset, but the day did not turn until it became dark enough for the first three night lights to be seen. In Mark 15:42, Joseph of Arimathea goes in the evening to ask for the body of Jesus. He can proceed with the burial but only until the first three night lights appear that mark the beginning of Sabbath. He did not have much time, which explains why the burial process was incomplete and required the women to return after the Sabbath ended.

- εἰσελθὼν 2nd aor. act. participle nom. sing. masc. of the deponent verb εἰσέρχομαι, agreeing with the subject of the main verb, "he" (Jesus) (temporal circumstantial participle which, in the aorist, expresses time previous to the time of the main verb) = "**after entering** or **upon entering**" or "**after he entered**" or "**he entered** (Decker 24)." For the designation of present tense but not the aorist tense of this verb as a deponent, see the comments on Mark 1:7, 9.

- εἰς τὴν συναγωγήν prepositional phrase (expressing motion toward and into) with εἰς + the accusative, here the acc. sing. fem. of the noun ἡ συναγωγή (object of the preposition) = "**into the synagogue.**" Note the repetition of εἰς in the prefix to the verb and the preposition. The repetition of the two may be accounted for by translating them "entering into."

The synagogue is the place where the people of the village and of the area around it would gather for worship and teaching on the Sabbath. The term synagogue originally referred to the group gathering (from συν-άγω= come together) and it also came to mean, as here, the building where the group gathered—a rectangular edifice with benches on three sides (architecturally referred to as a triclinium) and a front where the Torah scrolls were kept (if the village had such a scroll) and from where readers and teachers presented their readings and teachings to the gathering. The synagogue building served the purposes of worship and other functions for the village, such as community meetings and court.

- ἐδίδασκεν impf. act. ind. 3rd pers. sing. of the verb διδάσκω (an inceptive imperfect expressing the beginning of an action that will continue or an imperfect of action in progress) = "**he began to teach**" or "**he began teaching**" or "**he was teaching**" (Smyth 1900; Wallace 544–47). The imperfect could possibly be an iterative imperfect (Smyth, 1893; Wallace 546–47), thus describing activity that Jesus would regularly do on Sabbaths [see above under τοῖς σάββασιν] = "**he customarily taught.**" However, as we said above, this is unlikely because the passage is depicting a single occasion. Jesus was permitted to teach in the synagogue, because the synagogue service consisted of prayer, scripture reading, and teaching by anyone competent to give explanation or instruction.

<1:22> καὶ ἐξεπλήσσοντο ἐπὶ τῇ διδαχῇ αὐτοῦ· ἦν γὰρ διδάσκων αὐτοὺς ὡς ἐξουσίαν ἔχων καὶ οὐχ ὡς οἱ γραμματεῖς. = **And they were astonished at his teaching, for he was teaching them as one having authority and not as the scribes.**

καὶ ἐξεπλήσσοντο ἐπὶ τῇ διδαχῇ αὐτοῦ·

- καί coor. conj. (paratactic, connecting this sentence to the previous one) = "**and.**"

- ἐξεπλήσσοντο impf. mid. or pass. ind. 3rd pers. plur. of the verb ἐκπλήσσω (imperfect of a state of mind) = "**they (people) were astonished**" or "**they were astounded**" (Wallace 548). The verb ἐξεπλήσσοντο could also be an imperfect of description (Smyth, 1898; Wallace 543-44) or an imperfect of result (Smyth 1899), both of which would suggest that an outward expression of astonishment is being depicted rather than an inner state. Note the plural with no explicit subject (Decker 25; Williams 35-36). Mark uses several different words to depict the response of amazement, words that usually (but not always) imply an openness to Jesus but that by themselves do not describe someone who understands or who is necessarily able to follow Jesus (see Mark 1:27; 2:12; 5:20; 12:11). Here, ἐκπλήσσω is a strong word that literally means to "strike out of one's senses" or be "dumbfounded."

- ἐπὶ τῇ διδαχῇ prepositional phrase with ἐπί + the dative, here the dat. sing. fem. of the noun ἡ διδαχή (object of the preposition) = "**at**" or "**because of.**" The object of the preposition is perhaps a dative of respect = "**with respect to the teaching**" or "**by the teaching.**" Teaching here is probably not a reference to the content of the teaching as such, but serves rather as a verbal noun depicting his activity and manner of teaching. Some scholars associate this response to Jesus saying, "you have heard it said of old, ... But I say to you . . ." (e. g, Matt 5:21). However, there is no indication that this is implied by Mark's narrative.

- αὐτοῦ gen. sing. masc. of the 3rd pers. personal pronoun αὐτός, ή, ὁ (subjective genitive in which Jesus [αὐτοῦ] is the subject of the action implied in the noun [διδαχή] depicting an act of teaching) = "**at his teaching**" or "**by his teaching.**" Early in Mark, the amazement of the crowds focuses not so much on Jesus himself as on his teaching. As the story develops, people are amazed by Jesus himself (e. g. 4:41).

ἦν γὰρ διδάσκων αὐτοὺς

- γάρ postpositive subord. conj. (explanatory) = "**for.**" This clause explains why they were amazed.

- ἦν . . . διδάσκων combining the imperfect act. ind. 3rd pers. sing. of the verb εἰμί and the pres. act. nom. sing. masc. of the verb διδάσκω. (imperfect periphrastic participle construction) = "**he was teaching.**" A periphrasis is a construction that uses more words than needed to say what it intends to say. Here, Mark uses a form of εἰμί together with a participle instead of a simple one-word use of the imperfect. Together the two words of the construction are translated as an imperfect of διδάσκω. Periphrasis sometimes implies emphasis.

- αὐτούς acc. plur. masc. of the 3rd pers. personal pronoun αὐτός, ή, ὁ (direct object of the periphrastic construction) = "**them**" (the people in the synagogue).

ὡς ἐξουσίαν ἔχων,

- ὡς comparative adverb (manner) = "**as**" or "**like**." ὡς often precedes a circumstantial participle of manner.
- ἔχων pres. act. participle nom. sing. masc. of the verb ἔχω agreeing with the subject of the main verb above and equivalent to it (a circumstantial use of the participle without an article, explaining the manner of his teaching) = "**[as] one having**."
- ἐξουσίαν acc. sing. fem. of the noun ἡ ἐξουσία (direct object of the participle) = "**as one having authority**." In Mark, "having authority" refers to one who has been authorized to do something and who thereby bears the right and the power to speak (here command) and act on behalf of the authorizing agent.

The word ὡς may express the cause or purpose of Jesus' teaching and therefore state "the ground or belief on which the agent acts" (Smyth, 2086 and 2086b). That would be to say, Jesus teaches on the belief that he possesses authority from God = "**he was teaching them as if he had authority**" (with no implication that he did not have such authority).

καὶ οὐχ ὡς οἱ γραμματεῖς

- καί coord. conj. = "**and**." This conjunction connects the periphrastic ἦν διδάσκων with an elided ἦν διδάσκων negated by οὐχ = "**and not as the scribes [were teaching]**." In an antithesis, the negated verb is often elided, especially when it is the same as the verb in the positive statement.
- οὐχ adverbial negative used with the indicative mood = "**not**." Here οὐχ modifies an elided ἦν διδάσκων. Note also that οὐ has a χ ending before a word beginning with a vowel that has a hard or rough breathing.

- ὡς comparative adverb (manner) = "**as**" or "**like**." This is the same kind of ὡς clause that appears earlier in the sentence, except that this clause does not have a participle and is in the negative.

- οἱ γραμματεῖς nom. plur. masc. of the noun ὁ γραμματεύς = "**and not as the scribes** or **legal experts**" or "**teachers in the law**." The nominative οἱ γραμματεῖς would be seen as the subject of an elided verb διδάσκονται = "**[not as] the scribes teach**" = "**and [he was] not [teaching] as the scribes [teach]** (Decker 26)." Or οἱ γραμματεῖς could function as the predicate nominative of an elided ὤν (expressing cause or purpose), of which Jesus is the unexpressed subject. In this case, the parallel to the unexpressed ὤν is ἔχων = "**as if he has authority and not as if [he were] the scribes**."

It is difficult at this point in the episode to know what is meant by the contrast in authority between Jesus' teaching and that of the scribes. It has been suggested that scribes teach by citing precedents or authorization from scripture quotations while Jesus does not. Again, there is nothing to suggest this. Besides, Jesus does quote scripture elsewhere to support his actions (2:23–28). As this episode develops, the nature of Jesus' "teaching with authority" is expanded (with an exorcism) and clarified.

The scribes were, by definition, people who wrote (and read) and copied (in this context, the scriptures, referred to in Mark as "the writings"). By virtue of their skill, the scribes were therefore also experts in what they copied, namely the Law or Torah. Mark treats scribes either as an independent group or as members of one sect or another. In Mark, they are most closely associated with the Pharisees. These literate scribes are to be distinguished from village scribes who had only the rudimentary capacity to read and write such items as letters and contracts.

<1:23> καὶ εὐθὺς ἦν ἐν τῇ συναγωγῇ αὐτῶν ἄνθρωπος ἐν πνεύματι ἀκαθάρτῳ καὶ ἀνέκραξεν = **And immediately there was in their synagogue a man with an unclean spirit, and he cried out**

καὶ εὐθὺς ἦν ἐν τῇ συναγωγῇ αὐτῶν

- καί coor. conj. (paratactic, connecting this sentence to the previous one) = "**and**."

- εὐθύς adverb (temporal) = "**immediately**" or "**at once**." The adverb εὐθύς states the temporal relationship between the verb it modifies and the previous verb ἦν διδάσκων. Εὐθύς also sometimes serves in Mark to give coherence to the narrative (Decker 25). Here, εὐθὺς serves to connect what follows with the previous statement of the narrator, and it draws attention to the unusual and striking nature of the event to follow (Williams 36). It also shows the rapidity with which things happened after Jesus entered Capernaum.

- ἦν impf. act. ind. 3rd pers. sing. of the intransitive verb εἰμί = "**he was.**" Εἰμί can function either as an equative verb (to be) or as an active intransitive verb (to exist, to appear). Functioning here, as an intransitive verb, ἦν expresses active existence. Given the fact that it is modified by εὐθύς, it might best be translated in an active rather than a static way = "**immediately there appeared.**"

- ἐν τῇ συναγωγῇ prepositional phrase (expressing place or location) with ἐν + the dative, here the dat. sing. fem. of the noun ἡ συναγωγή (object of the preposition/dative of place where) = "**in the synagogue.**"

- αὐτῶν gen. plur. masc. of the 3rd pers. personal pronoun αὐτός, -ή, -ό (genitive of possession) = "**in their (the people of Capernaum) synagogue.**" The antecedent is *not* "the Jews," as though Mark were contrasting a Jewish from a Christian synagogue.

- ἄνθρωπος anarthrous nom. sing. masc. of the noun ὁ ἄνθρωπος (subject) = "**a man.**" Together with the verb, it may be translated "a man was" or "there was a man." The word ἄνθρωπος can function like the indefinite pronoun τίς and may be a substitute for it = "**a certain man**" or "**someone.**"

- ἐν πνεύματι ἀκαθάρτῳ prepositional phrase with ἐν + the dative, here the dat. sing. neut. of τὸ πνεῦμα, modified by the dat. sing. neut. of the adjective ἀκάθαρτος, ή, όν (object of the preposition) = "**with an unclean spirit.**" The preposition ἐν can mean "**with**" (dative of concomitant circumstances—Zerwick #116ff) or "**having**" or even, using principles of dynamic translation, "**possessed by**" or "**in the power of**" an unclean spirit (in which case πνεύματι might be the dative of thing possessed by, although that may be a doubtful category—Wallace 151; Decker 26–27; Williams 36). The preposition ἐν plus the dative could have the spatial sense of "in the sphere of the unclean spirit" (compare "in Christ").

The term "unclean spirit" is Mark's usual way to refer to a demon. An unclean spirit will defile the person who is possessed and perhaps defile others who have contact with such a one. Πνεύματι ἀκαθάρτῳ (ἀ-καθάρτῳ = not-clean or unclean spirit) is a contrast to the πνεῦμα ἅγιον (holy spirit) possessing Jesus. The contrast emphasizes that an unclean spirit brings defilement whereas God's spirit brings holiness. Placing the subject last in the sentence may give some suspense and emphasis to the surprising presence of such a person in the synagogue.

καὶ ἀνέκραξεν

- καί coord. conj. (paratactic, connecting ἀνέκραξεν to the previous verb ἦν) = "**and**."
- ἀνέκραξεν aor. act. ind. 3rd pers. sing. of the verb ἀνακράζω (punctiliar aorist) = "**he cried out**" or "**shouted**" or "**screamed**." This word is commonly used in connection with cries of fear. As such, it emphasizes the demon's terror and reinforces the expression of fear spoken by the frightened demon. This is a loud and vociferous conflict of power between Jesus and the unclean spirit.

<1:24> λέγων Τί ἡμῖν καὶ σοί, Ἰησοῦ Ναζαρηνέ; ἦλθες ἀπολέσαι ἡμᾶς; οἶδά σε τίς εἶ, ὁ ἅγιος τοῦ θεοῦ. = **saying, "What [do] you [have] against us, Jesus Nazarene? Did you come to destroy us? I know who you are, the holy one of God."**

- λέγων pres. act. participle nom. sing. masc. of the verb λέγω, agreeing with the subject of the main verb and depicting his action (temporal circumstantial participle which, as a present, expresses time concurrent with the time of the main verb) = "**saying**." Λέγων signals direct speech (called a recitative λέγων) and can be translated simply as a comma and quotation marks (, ". . ."). As such, the words that follow *are* the expression of what the unclean spirit cried out." Note that λέγων is the masculine (related to the man) rather than a neuter (which would be related to τὸ πνεῦμα). Λέγων thus portrays the possessed person speaking rather than the unclean spirit itself; nevertheless, he is obviously speaking under the control of the unclean spirit.

Τί ἡμῖν καὶ σοί, Ἰησοῦ Ναζαρηνέ;

- Τί acc. sing. neut. of the interrogative pronoun (introduces a question) = "**what**." Since τί is a nominative, it is the subject of an implied verb "to be" = "**What is with us and you.**"
- ἡμῖν dat. plur. of the 1st person personal pronoun ἐγώ (dative of respect) = "**us**." This dative can also be a dative of association, and the expression a dative of dissociation (Williams 36–37; Decker 27).
- καί coor. conj. (simple connective of the two datives) = "**and**."
- σοί dat. sing. of the 2nd pers. personal pronoun σύ (dative of respect) = "**you**." The verb ἐστιν is elided = "**it**" or "**is it?**" Coordinated with the previous dative, this dative can also be a dative of association or, as in this case, a dative of dissociation.

Taken as a whole, this question is an idiomatic expression involving two datives. The two pronouns can be taken either as two datives of respect ("What is it with respect to us and with respect to you") or two datives of possession ("What is ours and yours") (Wallace 149–51). Or they could be two datives of dissociation (Williams 36–37). Either way, the expression means literally "What [relationship] exists [between] us and you?" The sense of it may be conveyed by "What do we have in common?" or "What do you have to do with us?" or "Why are you interfering with us?" As a hostile expression (as it is here), it may be translated, "What is it between us and you?" or, more freely, "What do you have against us?" Note that, as a Markan two-step progression, this general question is followed immediately by a specific question, "Have you come to destroy us?" (see below).

- Ἰησοῦ voc. sing. masc. (direct address) = "**Jesus**."
- Ναζαρηνέ; voc. sing. masc. of the formal adjective Ναζαρηνός, -ή (substantive use of the adjective/ simple apposition to Ἰησου)~ = "**[Jesus,] the Nazarene**." Together the two function like a proper name (cf. Mark 10:44).

Note the semicolon at the end, which (in the edited punctuation of the Greek) serves as a question mark. This is the first of many questions in Mark with a variety of rhetorical functions. This question and the question to follow express fear on the part of the demon and demonstrate its hostile efforts to get power over Jesus by naming him.

ἦλθες ἀπολέσαι ἡμᾶς;

- ἦλθες 2nd aor. mid. or pass. ind. 2nd pers. sing. of the verb ἔρχομαι (global aorist depicting the whole emergence of Jesus' public ministry, here as an indicative in a simple question requesting information) = "**Did you (Jesus) come?**" Note how the word ἔρχομαι is sometimes used to express Jesus' purpose, for example, in such sayings as "That's why I came out" (1:38) and "I came not to call the righteous but the sinners" (2:17) (Decker 27).

- ἀπολέσαι aor. act. inf. of the verb ἀπόλλυμι (a complementary infinitive after ἔρχομαι, expressing purpose) = "**to destroy**" or "**in order to destroy.**" For the designation of the present tense but not the aorist tense of this verb as a deponent, see the comments on Mark 1:7, 9.

- ἡμᾶς acc. plur. of the 1st pers. personal pronoun (direct object of the infinitive) = "**us**" (the unclean spirits). In Mark, Jesus has authority to destroy demons but not to harm people. Mark uses the word ἀπόλλυμι to depict Jesus' actions against the demons, but he also uses it to portray the leaders' actions against Jesus (e.g. 3:6).

Double questions are common in Mark. These two particular questions together comprise a Markan two-step progression in which the first phrase is general ("What is between us and you?"), and the second phrase repeats the same idea with greater specificity ("Did you come to destroy us?"). Note how each question expresses the demon's fear of Jesus, with the second question expressing it specifically as the fear of destruction. Note also how the unclean spirit uses the plural ἡμᾶς as if the demon is speaking in a representative way for all of "us" demons. In Mark, this choice of the plural implies that this exorcism is not just an isolated exorcism but the beginning of an onslaught by this agent of the rule of God upon all demons. The second question ("Did you come to destroy us?") expresses a statement about the mission of Jesus, ironically, from the voice of an unclean spirit. Note how Jesus later destroys by drowning the legion of demons possessing the Gerasene demonic (5:1–13).

οἶδά σε τίς εἶ, ὁ ἅγιος τοῦ θεοῦ.

- οἶδα perf. act. ind. 1st. person sing. of the defective verb οἶδα (here as a present of state or condition) = "**I know.**" Only the perfect and pluperfect forms of οἶδα remain, and these function respectively as present and imperfect. The return to the singular ("*I know*") means the individual demon is now speaking for himself/itself in seeking to gain power over Jesus. This term for knowing expresses knowledge by seeing or experiencing.

- σε acc. sing. of the 2nd pers. personal pronoun (direct object of οἶδα) = "**you.**"

- τίς interrogative pronoun in the nom. sing. masc. of the interrogative pronoun τίς (the clause τίς εἶ is in apposition to σέ, τίς being in the nominative case as the predicate nominative of εἶ) = "**who.**"

- εἶ pres. ind. 2nd pers. sing. of the equative verb εἰμί = "**you are.**" The whole phrase (οἶδά σε τίς εἶ) can be rendered = "**I know you, who you are**" or simply "**I know who you are.**" This phrase is direct discourse after a verb of perception (οἶδα). The direct object followed by a ὅτι clause or (as here) its equivalent is a mixed construction (Moule 154).

Another way to construe this sentence is to consider οἶδα as a verb taking two objects. The first object is σε and the second is τίς εἶ, understood then as an object clause = "**I know you, [I know] who you are.**"

- ὁ ἅγιος nom. sing. masc. of the adjective ἅγιος, -η, -ον (substantive use of the article/simple apposition to the implied nominative subject of εἶ, i. e. "you") = "**the holy (one).**"

- τοῦ θεοῦ gen. sing. masc. of the noun ὁ θεός (genitive of relationship or genitive of origin) = "**the holy one of God**" or "**the Holy One from God.**"

The whole epithet could also be understood as a vocative (direct address), in which the nominative functions as a vocative. In such a case, calling Jesus "the holy one of God" answers the question, "Who are you?" This would be an emphatic vocative without the typical particle ὦ that is often used to give emphasis to a vocative (Wallace 68 n. 9).

The phrase "holy one of God" depicts Jesus as the agent chosen by God to be anointed with the "holy" spirit and to usher in God's rule. The adjective ἅγιος in the phrase "holy one of God" provides a contrast to the ἀκαθάρτῳ in "unclean spirit." It can be treated either as a title (Holy One of God) or as an epithet (the holy one of God).

Note that the two questions may parallel the two parts of the statement that follow, in which the demoniac answers his own question: "What do you have to do with us?" is answered by "I know you, who you are;" and "Did you come to destroy us?" is answered by "the "Holy One of God," that is, the "holy" spirit will destroy "unclean" spirits.

Note how, in Mark, the demon knows who Jesus is, because demons are minions of Satan, whom Jesus earlier confronted in the desert. They are frightened of Jesus because (by implication) they know that Jesus prevailed over Satan's efforts to tempt/test him and that he is therefore stronger than they are. Jesus will tell the unclean spirit to "keep quiet" (about Jesus' identity) and "get out." Note how the demons, who know Jesus, focus on who Jesus is, while the crowds, who do not know who he is, focus only on the nature of his teaching.

The demon has named Jesus twice ("Jesus Nazarene" and "Holy one of God"). Words were considered to have power, and naming Jesus was a way to get power over him (compare also the interchange between Jesus and the demon named "Legion" in 5:1–20). The whole sentence, "I know you, who you are, the holy one of God," is the demon's effort to control Jesus considering the threat to the demon implied in the two questions it posed to Jesus. The demons, however, are not powerful enough to make this happen. Note Jesus' parable of the strong man able to plunder Satan's house because he has already bound Satan (3:22–27).

<1:25> καὶ ἐπετίμησεν αὐτῷ ὁ Ἰησοῦς λέγων, Φιμώθητι καὶ ἔξελθε ἐξ αὐτοῦ.=
and Jesus rebuked it, saying, "Be muzzled and come out of him."

καὶ ἐπετίμησεν αὐτῷ ὁ Ἰησοῦς λέγων,

- καί coord. conj. (paratactic, connecting this sentence to the previous one) = "**and.**"
- ὁ Ἰησοῦς nom. sing. masc. of the proper name ὁ Ἰησοῦς (subject) = "**Jesus.**"
- ἐπετίμησεν aor. act. ind. 3rd pers. sing. of the verb ἐπιτιμάω (punctiliar aorist) = "**he**" (Jesus) "**rebuked**" or (given the command to "be quiet") it could mean "**censured.**" This is a strong term of repudiation.

- αὐτῷ dat. sing. neut. or masc. of the 3rd pers. personal pronoun αὐτός, -ή, -ό (direct object of ἐπιτιμάω in the dative, perhaps being dative under the influence of the prefix ἐπί) = "**it**" (Williams 37). The construction may also be designated as a dative complement of ἐπετίμησεν (Decker 28). The pronoun αὐτῷ is most likely in the neuter, for the antecedent of αὐτῷ is the unclean spirit (which is neuter in gender—τὸ πνεῦμα). Jesus rebukes demons. However, he also rebukes Peter when Peter, unwittingly representing Satan, rebukes Jesus for saying he will be rejected and executed (8:31–33). Rebuking here functions partly as command (see below 1:27) and partly as censure to "be muzzled," i.e for saying Jesus' identity aloud.

- λέγων pres. act. participle nom. sing. masc. of the verb λέγω (circumstantial participle which, as a present tense, expresses time concurrent with the time of the main verb and introduces what Jesus said in rebuking the unclean spirit) = "**saying**." This participle, λέγων, is called a recitative participle because it introduces direct speech and may be translated as quotation marks = ". . . ." What follows, then, are the words of Jesus' rebuke.

Φιμώθητι καὶ ἔξελθε ἐξ αὐτοῦ.

- Φιμώθητι aor. pass. imperative 2nd pers. sing. of the verb φιμόω (aorist imperative commanding a single action in this specific situation—Williams 37) = "**be muzzled**" (literally, like an ox—in its original meaning) or "**shut up**" or "**keep quiet**" or "**Silence!**" The command is intended to get the unclean spirit to stop blurting out Jesus' identity in public. The same word is used when Jesus commands the roiling sea to "Be quiet!" (4:39). The word serves to stifle the demon's effort to control Jesus. It also serves to keep the demon from making public Jesus' identity as the holy one of God.

- καί coor. conj. (simple connective between the two imperatives) = "**and**."

- ἔξελθε 2nd aor. act. imperative 2nd pers. sing. of the verb ἐξέρχομαι (aorist imperative commanding a single action in this specific situation, here a performance command in which the results occur at the same moment when the command is being made) = "**come out**." In Mark, the performance command of the imperative occurs often on the lips of Jesus. For the designation of the present tense but not the aorist tense of this verb as a deponent, see the comments on Mark 1:7, 9.

- ἐξ αὐτοῦ prepositional phrase with ἐξ + the genitive, here the gen. sing. masc. of the 3rd pers. personal pronoun αὐτός, -ή, -ό (object of the preposition/genitive of separation) = "**from him**" (i. e. from the person possessed). The preposition ἐκ becomes ἐξ before a word beginning with a vowel that has a soft breathing. Note the repetition of ἐκ in the prefix of the verb and the preposition. To account for the repetition in translation, one might render the phrase "Come *out from* him" or "Get *out of* him."

Note the parallels in which Jesus addresses the two concerns of the demon: (1) that the demons knew Jesus ("Be muzzled!") and (2) that the demon feared Jesus would destroy him ("And get out of him!").

<1:26> καὶ σπαράξαν αὐτὸν τὸ πνεῦμα τὸ ἀκάθαρτον καὶ φωνῆσαν φωνῇ μεγάλῃ ἐξῆλθεν ἐξ αὐτοῦ. = **And the unclean spirit, after convulsing him and crying in a loud cry, came out of him.**

καὶ σπαράξαν αὐτὸν τὸ πνεῦμα τὸ ἀκάθαρτον

- καί coord. conj. (paratactic, connecting this sentence to the previous one) = "**and.**"
- σπαράξαν aor. act. participle nom. sing. neut. of the verb σπαράσσω, agreeing with the subject of the sentence (temporal circumstantial participle which, as an aorist, expresses time previous to the time of the main verb) = "**after convulsing [him]**" or "**after shaking [him]**." Σπαράσσω is used in Mark to express the domination of a demon over a possessed person (also in Mark 9:26). In medical usage, it described the convulsive action of the stomach in retching.
- τὸ πνεῦμα τὸ ἀκάθαρτον nom. sing. neut. of the noun τὸ πνεῦμα modified in the attributive position by the nom. sing. neut. form of the adjective ἀκάθαρτος, η, ον (the subject of the sentence and the source of action for each of the two participles) = "**the unclean spirit.**" Here "*the* unclean spirit" is definite and refers to the specific unclean spirit possessing this man to which reference had already been made.
- αὐτόν acc. sing. masc. of the 3rd pers. personal pronoun αὐτός, -ή, -όν (direct object of the participle) = "**[after it shook] him**" (i. e. the man possessed).

καὶ φωνῆσαν φωνῇ μεγάλῃ

- καί coord. conj. (simple connector of two participles) = "**and**."
- φωνῆσαν aor. act. participle nom. sing. neut. of the verb φωνέω, agreeing with the subject ("the unclean spirit") of the sentence (a temporal circumstantial participle which, as an aorist, expresses time previous to the time of the main verb—paralleling the use of σπαράξαν) = "**and after crying out**" or "**after it screamed**" or "**yelling**" (Williams 37). Note how violent and vociferous is this conflict between Jesus and the demon.
- φωνῇ μεγάλῃ dat. sing. fem. of the noun ἡ φωνή modified by the dat. sing. fem. of the adjective μεγάς, μεγάλη, μέγα (together the two words form a dative of manner expressing *how* he cried out) = "**in a great cry**" or "**with a loud cry**" (Williams 37). Because the noun has the same root as the verb it modifies, it is also referred to as a cognate dative: "*cried* out in a loud *cry*" (Decker 28).

ἐξῆλθεν ἐξ αὐτοῦ.

- ἐξῆλθεν 2nd aor. act. ind. 3rd. pers. sing. of the verb ἐξέρχομαι (punctiliar aorist) = "**it (the unclean spirit) came out**." Since this follows immediately upon the yelling, the implication may be that the demon left the person through the mouth. For the designation of the present tense but not the aorist tense of this verb as a deponent, see the comments on Mark 1:7, 9.
- ἐξ αὐτοῦ prepositional phrase with ἐξ + the genitive, here the gen. sing. masc. of the 3rd pers. personal pronoun αὐτός, ἡ, ὁ (genitive of separation) = "**from him**" (the person possessed). The preposition ἐκ becomes ἐξ before a word beginning with a vowel that has a soft breathing. Note again the repetition of ἐκ in the prefix of the verb and the preposition. To account for the repetition in translation, one might render the phrase as "it came *out from* him" or "it came *out of* him." The repetition may reinforce the absolute nature of the expulsion of the demon from the man.

<1:27> καὶ ἐθαμβήθησαν ἅπαντες ὥστε συζητεῖν πρὸς ἑαυτοὺς λέγοντας, Τί ἐστιν τοῦτο; διδαχὴ καινὴ κατ' ἐξουσίαν; καὶ τοῖς πνεύμασιν τοῖς ἀκαθάρτοις ἐπιτάσσει, καὶ ὑπακούουσιν αὐτῷ. = **and all marveled with the result that**

they were discussing with each other, saying, "What is this? A new teaching with authority? He commands even the unclean spirits, and they obey him."

καὶ ἐθαμβήθησαν ἅπαντες

- καί coord. conj. (paratactic, connecting this sentence to the previous one) = "**and**."
- ἅπαντες nom. plur. masc. of the pronoun ἅπας, -ασα, -αν (subject). The word ἅπας is the strengthened form of πᾶς (all) = "**all together**" (Decker 29).
- ἐθαμβήθησαν aor. pass. ind. 3rd pers. plur. of the verb θαμβέω (global aorist depicting all the acts of amazement or a punctiliar aorist expressing the amazement of the crowd as one act) = "**were amazed**" or "**were astonished**." In Mark, θαμβέω expresses a positive response to Jesus. By itself, however, it expresses an inadequate response, because it does not encompass the understanding and the faithfulness needed to follow Jesus. Compare, for example, those in the parable of the Sower who receive the word but who ended up producing no fruit (4:14–20).

ὥστε συζητεῖν πρὸς ἑαυτοὺς λέγοντας,

- ὥστε subord. conj. (introduces a result clause + an infinitive) = "**so that**" or "**with the result [that]**." Here is a dependent result clause expressing the result of the action in the previous independent clause.
- συζητεῖν pres. act. infinitive of the verb συζητέω (infinitive in a result clause with ὥστε—with its unexpressed but implied subject being the same as the subject of the main clause) = "**[all] were discussing**" or "**[many] were questioning**" or "**debating**." The verb συζητέω may imply that there was a difference of opinion = "**so that [some] were arguing**" or "**so that [they] debated**."

The unexpressed subject of the infinitive may be the same as the subject of the main verb ("all"). Or the sentence may suggest that not all could speak at the same time and that the implied subject of the infinitive was different from the subject of the main verb. In this case, the implied subject of the infinitive might be construed as "many" = "**with the result that many were arguing**." Their dialogue is posed as a question.

- πρὸς ἑαυτοὺς prepositional phrase with πρός + the accusative, here acc. plur. masc. of the 3rd person reflexive pronoun ἑαυτοῦ, -ῆς, -οῦ (object of a preposition) = "**with one another**" or "**with each other**" or "**among themselves**." This prepositional phrase expresses reciprocal action between people as they question or debate what is happening (Williams 37).

- λέγοντας pres. act. acc. plur. masc. of the verb λέγω agreeing with the implied subject of the infinitive ("they" or "many"), which, if expressed, would be in the accusative [the subject of an infinitive is usually in the accusative] (a temporal circumstantial participle which, in the present tense, expresses time concurrent with the time of the main verb) = "**saying**." The words that follow *are* the expression of their questioning and not something separate or in addition to the debating about it. This participle, called a "recitative" λέγοντας because it introduces direct speech, may be translated as a comma and quotation marks = , ". . . ." This participle can also be considered redundant (Decker 29; Williams 37–38).

Τί ἐστιν τοῦτο;

- Τί nom. sing. neut. of the interrogative pronoun τίς (Decker 29). Contrast, for example, the disciples' question later in the storm at sea, "Who is this?" (4:41).

- ἐστιν pres. ind. 3rd pers. sing. of the equative verb εἰμί (functions equatively) = "**is**." The third person singular form of εἰμί is an enclitic, a word that goes without an accent.

- τοῦτο nom. sing. neut. of the demonstrative pronoun οὗτος, αὕτη, τοῦτο (predicate pronoun) = "**this**." The semicolon is a question mark. This is a direct question (Smyth 2636), which, in a straight forward way, seeks information (Smyth 2642; Wallace 449–50). It poses a conundrum.

διδαχὴ καινὴ κατ' ἐξουσίαν;

- διδαχὴ καινὴ anarthrous nom. sing. fem. of the noun ἡ διδαχή, modified by the nom. sing. fem. of the adjective καινός, -ή, -όν (apposition or predicate nominative) = "**a new teaching**." Καινή expresses the quality of the teaching as well as the temporal newness of it. Διδαχή here expresses the act of teaching more than the content of what is taught.

The syntax of διδαχὴ καινή may be taken in one of two ways. (1) It may be in apposition to τοῦτο, in which case, there is only one sentence here, to be translated as, "What is this, a new teaching with authority?" (2) Or διδαχὴ καινη may be taken as the predicate nominative of a verb that is elided (Decker 29), probably ἐστίν or ἐστιν τοῦτο, to be translated as, "What is this? [Is it] a new teaching with authority?" Note the asyndeton, in which there is no connecting particle between these two questions.

Also notice that this a Markan two-step progression in which the first part ("What is this?") is general, And the second step is specific (Is this a new teaching with authority?).

- κατ' ἐξουσίαν; prepositional phrase with κατά + the accusative, here acc. sing. fem. of the noun ἡ ἐξουσία = "**according to authority**" or "**with authority**" (indicating the manner of the act of teaching). The phrase is an adverbial prepositional phrase expressing the manner of Jesus' activity in teaching, because he makes commands! (Decker 30; Williams 38). Some commentators consider "with authority" to be part of the following sentence rather than part of this question = "... **a new teaching? With authority he commands even . . . .**" The alpha at the end of κατά is elided before words beginning with a vowel with soft breathing. The elision is signified in translation by an apostrophe. The semi-colon at the end of the sentence is the editorial equivalent of a question mark.

καὶ τοῖς πνεύμασι τοῖς ἀκαθάρτοις ἐπιτάσσει,

- καί adverb modifying the verb ἐπιτάσσει (ascensive use of an adverb) = "**even.**" Here it strengthens and intensifies the verb.
- τοῖς πνεύμασι τοῖς ἀκαθάρτοις dat. plur. neut. of the noun τὸ πνεῦμα, modified in the attributive position by the dat. plur. neut of the adjective ἀκάθαρτος, -η, ον (dative as direct object/complement of verbs of commanding—Smyth 1460, 1464; cf. Wallace 171–72), the case being influenced in part by the prefix ἐπί) = "**the unclean spirits.**" Mark has the crowds say, "He commands *even [also?]* the unclean spirits." This construction may suggest that he performed healings in his teaching at the beginning of the episode and is now *also* commanding the

unclean spirits? More likely, however, it is simply an emphatic way of making the point.

- ἐπιτάσσει pres. act. ind. of the verb επιτάσσω (global present covering all Jesus' actual and potential acts of commanding) = "**he commands.**"

καὶ ὑπακούουσιν αὐτῷ.

- καί coor. conj. (paratactic, connecting this sentence to the previous one) = "**and.**"
- ὑπακούουσιν pres. act. ind. 3rd pers. sing. of the verb ὑπακούω (global present covering all acts of response to all Jesus' commands) = "**they (the unclean spirits) obey**" or "**they are subject to him.**" There is no suggestion that the spirits obeyed willingly. Most often, neuter plural subjects take a singular verb. Therefore, one might have expected a singular verb after this implied neuter plural subject of ἀκούω. However, animate things (here the "spirits") in the neuter plural may take a plural subject.
- αὐτῷ dat. sing. masc. of the 3rd pers. personal pronoun αὐτός, -ή, -ό (dative as direct object/complement to the verb of obedience) = "**him**" (Jesus). The crowd generalizes this single exorcism by acknowledging that Jesus has universal authority over all unclean spirits. Note also how the "commanding" and "obeying" give content to the concept of "a new teaching" that is done "with authority."

It is not clear if the crowd's comments are two questions followed by a statement or one question with two parts followed by a statement. If there are two questions represented here in verse 27, then there are four questions altogether in this episode, two spoken by the unclean spirit and two spoken by the crowd. The two questions spoken by the demons express their fear of and hostility toward Jesus. The two questions spoken by the crowd express and explain their amazement at Jesus' teaching and action. Thus, there seems to be a parallel in structure as well as content between the two questions + a statement put by the demon, on the one hand, and the two questions + a statement put by the onlookers, on the other hand.

What do you have against us, Jesus Nazarene?	What is this?
Did you come to destroy us?	A new teaching with authority?
I know who you are, the holy one of God.	He gives orders even to the unclean spirits, and they obey him.

Questions—real questions, rhetorical questions, accusatory questions, exclamatory questions—are a common and significant part of Mark's narrative. Mark uses questions to reveal character, intensify conflict, advance the plot, and foster an ethos of mystery. Careful attention to this feature of his language will bear much fruit in the study of Mark.

<1:28> καὶ ἐξῆλθεν ἡ ἀκοὴ αὐτοῦ εὐθὺς πανταχοῦ εἰς ὅλην τὴν περίχωρον τῆς Γαλιλαίας. = **And the report about him went out immediately everywhere, into the whole surrounding countryside of Galilee.**

καὶ ἐξῆλθεν ἡ ἀκοὴ αὐτοῦ εὐθὺς

- καί coord. conj. (paratactic, connecting this sentence to the previous one) = "**and.**"
- ἡ ἀκοή nom. sing. fem. of the noun ἡ ἀκοή (subject). The noun ἀκοή expresses a passive sense of what is heard = "**report.**"
- αὐτοῦ, gen. sing. masc. of the 3rd pers. personal pronoun αὐτός, ή, ό (objective genitive, depicting Jesus as the object of the action implied in the verbal noun ἀκοή) =" **the hearing about him**" (literally) or "**the report of/about him.**"
- ἐξῆλθεν 2nd aor. act. ind. 3rd pers. sing. of the verb ἐξέρχομαι (global aorist describing the whole process of many acts by which the report went out and was heard) = "**went out.**" For the designation of the present tense but not the aorist tense of this verb as a deponent, see the comments on Mark 1:7, 9.
- εὐθύς adverb (temporal) = "**at once**" or "**immediately.**" Εὐθύς here emphasizes the rapidity with which the word about Jesus spread as a consequence of Jesus' exorcism of the unclean spirit. This is the third occurrence of εὐθύς in this episode.

πανταχοῦ εἰς ὅλην τὴν περίχωρον τῆς Γαλιλαίας.

- πανταχοῦ adverb (place, modifying the main verb ἐξῆλθεν and explaining where the report went out) = "**everywhere**" or "**in all directions.**"
- εἰς ὅλην τὴν περίχωρον prepositional phrase (expressing motion toward and into) with εἰς + the accusative, here the acc. sing. fem. of the adjective περίχωρος, -η, -ον, here used as a substantive and modified in the predicate position by the acc. sing. fem. of the pronominal adjective

- ὅλος, -η, -ον. (substantive use of the adjective/object of the preposition) = "**the surrounding countryside [or land] as a whole** or **the entire neighboring region**." The article and adjective are feminine, because ἡ χώρα (= countryside, region) or ἡ γῆ (= land) is the unexpressed noun that the adjective modifies. When ὅλος modifies in attributive position, unlike here, it means "the whole [countryside]" as the sum of all its parts. When ὅλος modifies in the predicate position, as here, it means "[the countryside] as a whole" with each of its individual parts emphasized (Smyth, 1174–75).

- τῆς Γαλιλαίας gen. sing. fem. of the proper noun ἡ Γαλιλαία. There are three choices here for the syntax of the genitive. (1) τῆς Γαλιλαίας could be a partitive genitive, by which Galilee would be the whole of which the surrounding countryside of Capernaum is a part = "**[the whole surrounding countryside] in Galilee**" or "**the whole neighboring territory [which is part] of Galilee**." (2) Or, it could be a genitive determined by the prefix περί (when περί occurs as a preposition, it takes the genitive), by which Galilee would be the center around which there were other territories = "**the territory surrounding Galilee**" (such as Syria). (3) More likely, it is a genitive of apposition (or epexegetical genitive, as it is referred to by BDAG under περίχωρος), by which the "surrounding territory" *is* "Galilee" = "**the surrounding land, [which is] Galilee**" (compare, in English, how "the state of Wisconsin"= "the state, Wisconsin") (Decker 30–31).

Note the Markan two step progression: "everywhere" is the first general step, which is then followed by the second more precise step, "into the whole surrounding countryside of Galilee." The second step specifies what is meant by "everywhere."

WHAT FOLLOWS

This episode is part of a series of episodes, all held together by temporal markers that cover a continuous period in the village of Capernaum—from Jesus' Sabbath activities on one day to Jesus' praying in the desert on the following morning. After teaching and driving out a demon in this episode, Jesus heals Simon's mother-in-law, and then, when the Sabbath is over, he heals many people and drives out many demons, and finally, after prayer the next morning, he announces that he will go to the other villages in

Galilee to proclaim and drive out demons. The structure of these episodes suggests this meaning: having proclaimed, taught, healed, and exorcised demons in Capernaum, Jesus then determines to go and do the same things throughout all Galilee. Mark does not recount what happens in these other villages of Galilee. He does not need to, because he has set the pattern in Capernaum and then simply states that Jesus did the same elsewhere.

5

Jesus the Healer
Mark 1:29–39

PREVIEW

Along with the exorcism in the synagogue (1:21–28), the events narrated here represent a day spent in the village of Capernaum. Jesus proclaims, teaches with authority, drives out demons, and heals the sick. Early the next morning, in prayer, he determines to go on to the other villages of Galilee to repeat what he has done in Capernaum. Wherever he goes, as the agent of the rule of God, Jesus brings healing of illnesses and liberation from demons, and his activity generates wide popular support.

‹1:29› Καὶ εὐθὺς ἐκ <u>τῆς συναγωγῆς</u> <u>ἐξελθόντες</u>	And immediately <u>after coming out</u> of <u>the synagogue</u>
ἦλθον εἰς <u>τὴν οἰκίαν</u> Σίμωνος καὶ Ἀνδρέου	they went into <u>the house</u> of Simon and Andrew
μετὰ Ἰακώβου καὶ Ἰωάννου.	with James and John.
‹1:30› ἡ δὲ πενθερὰ Σίμωνος κατέκειτο <u>πυρέσσουσα</u>,	Now the mother-in-law of Simon was lying down <u>because she had a fever</u>
καὶ εὐθὺς λέγουσιν αὐτῷ περὶ αὐτῆς.	and immediately they speak to him about her
‹1:31› καὶ προσελθὼν	and after approaching (her)
<u>ἤγειρεν</u> αὐτὴν	he <u>raised</u> her <u>up</u>
κρατήσας τῆς χειρός·	by grasping her hand.

καὶ ἀφῆκεν αὐτὴν <u>ὁ πυρετός</u>,	And <u>the fever</u> left her
καὶ <u>διηκόνει</u> αὐτοῖς.	and she began <u>serving</u> them.

⟨1:32⟩ Ὀψίας δὲ γενομένης, Now after evening came,
    ὅτε ἔδυ ὁ ἥλιος,   when the sun set,
ἔφερον πρὸς αὐτὸν they brought to him
    πάντας <u>τοὺς κακῶς ἔχοντας</u>   all <u>those who were sick</u>
    καὶ <u>τοὺς δαιμονιζομένους</u>·   and <u>those possessed by demons</u>.
⟨1:33⟩ καὶ ἦν ὅλη ἡ πόλις ἐπισυνηγμένη πρὸς τὴν θύραν. And the whole city was gathered at the door.
⟨1:34⟩ καὶ ἐθεράπευσεν πολλοὺς <u>κακῶς ἔχοντας</u> And he healed many <u>who were sick</u>
    ποικίλαις <u>νόσοις</u>   with various <u>illnesses</u>,
    καὶ <u>δαιμόνια</u> πολλὰ ἐξέβαλεν   and he drove out many <u>demons</u>.
καὶ οὐκ ἤφιεν λαλεῖν <u>τὰ δαιμόνια</u>, And he would not permit <u>the demons</u> to speak
    ὅτι ᾔδεισαν αὐτόν.   because they knew him.

⟨1:35⟩ Καὶ πρωῒ ἔννυχα λίαν And very early, while still quite dark,
    ἀναστὰς   after arising
<u>ἐξῆλθεν</u> he <u>came out</u>
καὶ <u>ἀπῆλθεν</u> εἰς ἔρημον τόπον and <u>went off</u> to a desert place
κἀκεῖ προσηύχετο. and there was praying.
⟨1:36⟩ καὶ κατεδίωξεν αὐτὸν Σίμων And Simon and those with him
    καὶ οἱ μετ' αὐτοῦ,   tracked him down,
⟨1:37⟩ καὶ εὗρον αὐτὸν and they found him
καὶ λέγουσιν αὐτῷ and they say to him,
    ὅτι Πάντες ζητοῦσίν σε.   [that] "All are seeking you."
⟨1:38⟩ καὶ λέγει αὐτοῖς, And he says to them,
Ἄγωμεν ἀλλαχοῦ εἰς τὰς ἐχομένας κωμοπόλεις, "Let us go elsewhere,
    to the neighboring towns,
    ἵνα καὶ ἐκεῖ <u>κηρύξω</u>·   in order that also there I might
                <u>proclaim</u>,
εἰς τοῦτο γὰρ <u>ἐξῆλθον</u>. for on account of that I <u>came out</u>."
⟨1:39⟩ καὶ <u>ἦλθεν</u> <u>κηρύσσων</u> εἰς <u>τὰς συναγωγὰς</u> αὐτῶν And he <u>went</u> proclaiming in their <u>synagogues</u>,
    εἰς ὅλην τὴν Γαλιλαίαν   in the whole of Galilee,
    καὶ <u>τὰ δαιμόνια</u> <u>ἐκβάλλων</u>.   and <u>driving out</u> <u>the demons</u>.

WORD FIELD AND MOTIFS

The framing word field for this episode is (1) "journey." Within this frame occur other word fields: (2) "illness and healing;" (3) "possession and exorcism;" (4) "prayer and mission;" and (5) "popular response."

"Journey"

This episode represents a transition from a day in the activity of Jesus in one place (Capernaum) to a movement throughout other villages of Galilee. Jesus "goes out from the synagogue" (ἐκ τῆς συναγωγῆς) and "into the house of Simon and Andrew" (εἰς τὴν οἰκίαν Σίμωνος καὶ Ἀνδρέου). That evening the people of Capernaum bring their sick and possessed. Then early in the morning, while still quite dark, he "goes off to a deserted place" (ἀπῆλθεν εἰς ἔρημον τόπον) where he prays and determines to "go elsewhere, to the next towns" (ἀλλαχοῦ εἰς τὰς ἐχομένας κωμοπόλεις). The narrator concludes with the note that Jesus went proclaiming "in their synagogues, in the whole of Galilee" (εἰς τὰς συναγωγὰς αὐτῶν εἰς ὅλην τὴν Γαλιλαίαν). This transition sets the tone for the travel Jesus will do throughout the subsequent narrative as he pursues "the way" of God.

"Prayer and Calling"

The transitional movement in the journey is expressed by the word field of "prayer and calling." Jesus makes the decision to move on to other places while he was in prayer (κἀκεῖ προσηύχετο). The implication is that he is not called to stay in one place and enjoy the popularity there. Rather, his purpose was to proclaim, heal, and exorcize in many places. And so he tells his disciples of his decision to proclaim also in the neighboring towns, "for that is why I came out" (εἰς τοῦτο γὰρ ἐξῆλθον). The concept of "coming" is a significant aspect of Jesus' calling in Mark. A tracing of this word in Mark's narrative through the use of the concordance will yield many insights about Mark's portrayal of Jesus' mission.

"Illness and Healing" and "Possession and Exorcism"

Mark identifies the two major actions of Jesus' mission: healing and exorcism. These actions are expressions of the rule of God. Here, Simon's mother-in-law is "lying down because of a fever" (κατέκειτο πυρέσσουσα). Jesus "approached her" (καὶ προσελθὼν) and then "raised her up by grasping her hand" (ἤγειρεν αὐτὴν κρατήσας τῆς χειρός). "The fever left her" (καὶ ἀφῆκεν αὐτὴν ὁ πυρετός) and "she began serving them" (καὶ διηκόνει αὐτοῖς). Note how Jesus' healing leads to serving. The rule of God brings people to wholeness in order that they might serve one another. Serving is an activity that is integral to discipleship for all who follow Jesus (10:43–45). Note that when he heals on the Sabbath, as he does here and as he does in the case of the man with the withered hand (3:1–6), Jesus takes full responsibility for the healing so as not to implicate a supplicant in the illegality of requesting that Jesus work on the Sabbath.

When the Sabbath passes at sunset, people are able to travel, and the whole city gathers at the door. The villagers bring "all those who are sick" (πάντας τοὺς κακῶς ἔχοντας) and "those possessed of demons" (καὶ τοὺς δαιμονιζομένους). And Jesus "healed many who were sick with various illnesses" (καὶ ἐθεράπευσεν πολλοὺς κακῶς ἔχοντας ποικίλαις νόσοις) and "he drove out many demons" (καὶ δαιμόνια πολλὰ ἐξέβαλεν). The last note of the episode (1:29) brings readers back around to the beginning of the sequence of events in Capernaum. The narrator tells us that Jesus went proclaiming "in their synagogues" (εἰς τὰς συναγωγὰς αὐτῶν) throughout all Galilee and "driving out the demons" (καὶ τὰ δαιμόνια ἐκβάλλων). This recalls for us the exorcism in the synagogue at Capernaum that began the day (1:21–28).

"Popular Support"

In general, Mark portrays three responses to Jesus' activity: following (for those whom he calls to be disciples); enthusiastic support from the people; and antagonistic opposition from the leaders. In this episode, we see that Jesus' exorcism in the synagogue and his healing in the house have engendered a widespread popular response that leads the villagers to bring many people for healing and exorcism. As the narrator puts it: "And the whole city gathered at the door" (καὶ ἦν ὅλη ἡ πόλις ἐπισυνηγμένη πρὸς τὴν θύραν). This popular response is reinforced by the depiction of Simon and those with him saying to Jesus that "Everyone is looking for you" (Πάντες ζητοῦσίν σε). When the narrator comments at the end of the episode that Jesus went proclaiming and exorcising "in their synagogues, in all Galilee" (εἰς τὰς συναγωγὰς αὐτῶν, εἰς ὅλην τὴν Γαλιλαίαν), the implication is that the same pattern of action followed by a huge popular response will be repeated wherever Jesus goes.

Several minor motifs relate to this: First, Jesus' unwillingness to stay in Capernaum and enjoy the fact that "everyone is looking for you" suggests that he will not be motivated by the response of people (either for or against). Rather, he will have his own inner direction drawn from God in prayer. As the Pharisees will accurately say to him later, "You do not look to the reactions of people but truthfully teach the way of God" (12:14). Secondly, the disciples themselves are in fact enamored with this public response and want Jesus to stay in Capernaum because of it. This is the first suggestion in Mark's narrative that the disciples may not share the same goals as Jesus. Later we learn how much they are motivated by a desire for public honor in their following of Jesus (e. g. 9:34; 10:37). Finally, in the presence of the crowds, Jesus has a concern to keep his identity secret. Jesus "would not permit the demons to speak" (καὶ οὐκ ἤφιεν λαλεῖν τὰ δαιμόνια), "because they knew him" (ὅτι ᾔδεισαν αὐτόν). This repeats Jesus' earlier effort to tell the unclean spirit in the synagogue to "Be quiet," because the demon threatened to reveal Jesus' identity as the "Holy One of God" (1:24). These are the first explicit expressions of the messianic secret motif in Mark.

STRUCTURE

We may discern three episodes (almost small enough to be called vignettes or scenes) in this pericope (Noble 276, 384, 290). They are the last three in a series of four related episodes.

1 1: 21–28 (teaching/exorcising an unclean spirit)

2. 1:29–31 (healing Simon's mother-in-law)

3. 1:32–34 (healing and exorcising after sunset)

4. 1:35–39 (Jesus at prayer, leading to activity in other villages of Galilee)

All four episodes are held together by spatial and temporal markers. Spatially, they all take place in and around Capernaum. Temporally, they take place on and just after the Sabbath. The actions begin with daytime activities in the synagogue on the Sabbath, continue in the house of Simon and Andrew with the healing of Simon's mother-in-law, are followed by healing and exorcisms on the same evening at the house of Simon and Andrew when the Sabbath is over, and finally on the next morning Jesus goes to prayer in a deserted place and decides to move on. In so doing, Jesus expresses a determination to do the same things in other villages throughout Galilee that he has done in Capernaum, and then he proceeds to do so.

Setting:
<1:29> And immediately coming out of the synagogue
    they went into the house of Simon and Andrew
        with James and John.

Situation:
<1:30> Now the mother-in-law of Simon was lying down   a
    feverish   b

Problem:
and immediately they tell him about her,

Reply to the problem:
<1:31> and approaching (her)   a
    he raised her up
        by grasping her hand.

Result:
And the fever left her   b

Consequence:
and she began serving them.

Setting:
<1:32> Now when it became evening
    when the sun set

Situation:
they brought to him
    all those who were sick   a
    and those possessed by demons.   b
<1:33> And the whole city was gathered at the door.

Reply to the situation:
<1:34> And he healed many who were sick   a
    with various illnesses,
and he drove out many demons.   b

Consequence:
And he would not permit the demons to speak
        because they knew him.

Setting:
<1:35> And early, while still quite dark, after arising
   he came out
   and went off to a desert place

Situation:
   and there was praying.

Problem:
<1:36> And Simon and those with him tracked him down,
<1:37> and they found him
and they say to him
   [that] "All are seeking you."

Reply to the problem:
<1:38> And he says to them,
   "Let's go elsewhere, to the next towns,   a
      in order that I might proclaim there too,   b
      for on account of that I came out."

Consequence:
<1:39> And he went proclaiming in their synagogues,   b
   into the Galilee as a whole,   a
   and driving out the demons.

Note how the patterns of repetition in the sequence of events in Capernaum emphasize the importance of exorcism and healing:

   (a) Jesus exorcises a demon from a demoniac (1:21–28)

   (b) and he heals a woman who is sick (1:29–31).

   (b) People bring to him all those who are sick (1:33)

   (a) and those possessed of demons (1:33).

   (b) And he heals many who are sick of various illnesses (1:34)

   (a) and he drives out many demons (1:34).

The pattern first gives a description of one person being exorcized and one person being healed. Then it describes the sick and possessed who come to Jesus. Finally, it gives a description of many healings and many exorcisms. At the end of the episode, there is a general summary of the same activity to be taking place in other villages. There is no need for the narrator to repeat the specific activity for every village, because we readers can infer that it basically replicates the activity in Capernaum. The last episode also places all this activity within the framework of proclaiming (the rule of God). This kind of repetition is common in oral narration.

LINGUISTIC COMMENTARY

<1:29> Καὶ εὐθὺς ἐκ τῆς συναγωγῆς ἐξελθόντες ἦλθον εἰς τὴν οἰκίαν Σίμωνος καὶ Ἀνδρέου μετὰ Ἰακώβου καὶ Ἰωάννου = **And immediately after coming out of the synagogue, they went into the house of Simon and Andrew with James and John.**

Καὶ εὐθὺς ἐκ τῆς συναγωγῆς ἐξελθόντες

- Καί coord. conj. (paratactic, connects this sentence to the preceding one) = "**and.**"

- εὐθύς adverb (temporal) = "**immediately**" or "**at once.**" As an adverb, εὐθύς modifies the verb ἦλθον and temporally relates the action of this verb to the action expressed by the participle ἐξελθόντες. In this context, εὐθύς expresses the urgency of Jesus' activity. Together with καί, εὐθύς clarifies that it will still be the Sabbath when Jesus heals Simon's mother-in-law.

- ἐκ τῆς συναγωγῆς prepositional phrase with ἐκ + the genitive, here gen. sing. fem. of the noun ἡ συναγωγή (genitive of origin) = "**from the synagogue.**" (On the synagogue, see 1:21).

- ἐξελθόντες 2nd aor. mid. (in form) participle nom. plur. masc. of the verb ἐξέρχομαι, agreeing with the nom. plur. masc. of the subject of the main verb that follows (temporal circumstantial participle which, as an aorist, expresses time previous to the time of the main verb) = "**after coming out of**" or "**after they had come out of.**" If this participle is treated as a "participle of attendant circumstances," the best translation would be "**they came out and went.**" Note the repetition of ἐκ in the preposition and in the prefix of the verb. The force of this repetition may be captured by translating them "out from." For the designation of the present tense but not the aorist tense of this verb as a deponent, see the comments on Mark 1:7, 9.

ἦλθον εἰς τὴν οἰκίαν Σίμωνος καὶ Ἀνδρέου μετὰ Ἰακώβου καὶ Ἰωάννου.

- ἦλθον 2nd aor. mid. (in form) ind. 3rd person plur. of the deponent verb ἔρχομαι (punctiliar aorist) = "**they came.**" This is one of Mark's plural verbs in which the subject is unspecified (Williams 38). As such, it is not clear who is "coming out from" the synagogue, presumably Jesus, Simon, and Andrew, followed by James and John. This would connect the subject of this verb to the group who entered the synagogue together (1:21).

- εἰς τὴν οἰκίαν prepositional phrase of place (expressing motion toward and into) with εἰς + the accusative, here acc. sing. fem. of the noun ἡ οἰκία = "**into the house.**" Note the movement from synagogue to house that foreshadows a general movement in the narrative from activity in synagogues to activity in houses.
- Σίμωνος καὶ Ἀνδρέου gen. sing. masc. form of two proper names ὁ Σίμων and ὁ Ἀνδρέας respectively, connected by a καί (possessive genitive) = "**of Simon and Andrew.**" Note that it is a house in which both brothers reside. Given the order of naming, Simon is probably the eldest.
- μετὰ Ἰακώβου καὶ Ἰωάννου prepositional phrase with μετά (expressing association) + the genitive, here gen. sing. masc. of two formal names ὁ Ἰάκωβος and ὁ Ἰωάννης, connected by καί (making it a compound object of the preposition/genitive of association) = "**with James and John**" or "**followed by James and John.**" Note how the implied association of the two pairs of fishing partners continues after they begin to follow Jesus. Again, given the order of naming, James is probably the eldest.

<1:30> ἡ δὲ πενθερὰ Σίμωνος κατέκειτο πυρέσσουσα, καὶ εὐθὺς λέγουσιν αὐτῷ περὶ αὐτῆς. = **Now the mother-in-law of Simon was lying down because she had a fever, and immediately they speak to him about her.**

ἡ δὲ πενθερὰ Σίμωνος κατέκειτο πυρέσσουσα,

- δὲ postpositive coord. conj. (paratactic, connecting this sentence to the preceding one and suggesting the introduction of new information) = "**and**" or "**now.**"
- ἡ πενθερά nom. sing. fem. of the noun ἡ πενθερά (subject) = "**the mother-in-law.**"
- Σίμωνος, gen. sing. masc. of the proper name ὁ Σίμων (genitive of relationship) = "**[the mother-in-law] of Simon**" (Williams 38). It is

unusual for a mother-in-law to reside in the house of a son-in-law. The implication may be that Simon has taken her into his home (perhaps to care for the illness or because she is a widow with no sons of her own).

- κατέκειτο impf. mid. (in form) ind. 3rd person sing. of the deponent verb κατακείμαι (imperfect of an ongoing state) = "**was lying down.**" The prefix κατα- emphasizes her prone position resulting from the illness. Many categorize this verb as deponent, but a person cannot perform the action of lying down without being affected by that action. Hence, the middle voice in Greek is appropriate to express such an action even though an active voice translation is needed in English. See comments on deponent verbs on Mark 1:4.

- πυρέσσουσα pres. act. participle nom. sing. fem. of the verb πυρέσσω, agreeing with ἡ πενθέρα (a present circumstantial participle of time which, in the present, expresses action concurrent with the time of the main verb) = "**fevering**" or "**having a fever**" or "**with a fever.**" The root of πυρέσσω means "fire." The participle may be causal = [was lying down] "**because she had a fever**" (Decker 32; Williams 38).

καὶ εὐθὺς λέγουσιν αὐτῷ περὶ αὐτῆς.

- καί coord. conj. (paratactic, connects this sentence to the preceding one) = "**and.**"

- εὐθύς adverb (temporal) = "**immediately**". Here εὐθύς modifies the verb λέγουσιν and expresses the urgency with which they reported the illness.

- λέγουσιν pres. act. ind. 3rd person plur. of the verb λέγω (historical present) = "**they tell**" or "**they told**" or "**they speak to**" (Williams 38). The unspecified plural subject of the verb most likely refers to "Simon and Andrew." The presence of the historical present makes the narrative more vivid and immediate, especially in an oral presentation.

- αὐτῷ dat. sing. masc. of the 3rd person personal pronoun αὐτός, -ή, -ό (indirect object) = "**to him**" (Jesus).

- περὶ αὐτῆς prepositional phrase with περί + the genitive, here the gen. sing. fem. of the 3rd person personal pronoun αὐτός, -ή, -ό = "**concerning her**" or "**about her**" (the mother-in-law of Simon).

<1:31> καὶ προσελθὼν ἤγειρεν αὐτὴν κρατήσας τῆς χειρός· καὶ ἀφῆκεν αὐτὴν ὁ πυρετὸς καὶ διηκόνει αὐτοῖς = **and after approaching her he raised her up by grasping her hand, and the fever left her and she began serving them.**

καὶ προσελθὼν ἤγειρεν αὐτὴν κρατήσας τῆς χειρός·

- καί coor. conj. (paratactic, connects this sentence to the preceding one) = "**and**."

- προσελθών 2nd aor. act. participle nom. sing. masc. of the verb προσέρχομαι agreeing with the subject of the main verb "he" (Jesus) (a temporal circumstantial participle which, in the aorist, expresses time previous to the time of the main verb) = "**after approaching**" (her) or "**after he approached her**" or (simply) "**approaching her**" or (making the participle parallel to the main verb) "**he approached her and . . . .**" προσέρχομαι could also be rendered "**coming to**" or "**drawing near**." For the designation of the present tense but not the aorist tense of this verb as a deponent, see the comments on Mark 1:7, 9.

- ἤγειρεν aor. act. ind. 3rd person sing. of the verb ἐγείρω (punctiliar aorist) = "**he raised**." The word ἐγείρω is used often to refer to the consequences of a healing, of which Simon's mother-in-law is one example (Mark 2:9, 11, 12; 3:3; 5:41; 9:27). It suggests that God brings new life out of illness and that healing is therefore like a resurrection. This verb also depicts actual acts of resurrection (Mark 6:14, 16; 14:28; and 16:6).

- αὐτήν acc. sing. fem. of the 3rd pers. personal pronoun αὐτός, -ή, -ό (direct object) = "**her**."

- κρατήσας aor. act. participle nom. sing. masc. of the verb κρατέω, agreeing with the subject of the main verb "he" (Jesus) (circumstantial participle of means) = "**by grasping**" or "**by seizing**" or "**by taking hold of**." Some understand this participle as temporal (Decker 32; Williams 38–39), but a participle of means fits the context better. There is here a typical Markan accumulation of participles, in this case, one before and one after the main verb.

Note that, in Mark, Jesus heals in a variety of ways. Here he simply uses the gesture of helping her up. An ordinary action such as this serves to accomplish the healing without constituting work on the Sabbath. Compare

Jesus the Healer

the healing of the man with the withered hand, where he effects the healing simply by saying, "Stretch out the hand" (3:1–6).

- τῆς χειρός gen. sing. fem. of the noun ἡ χείρ (genitive instead of accusative to express the direct object or complement after certain verbs of sensing, here "grasping"/partitive genitive). The article functions here as a possessive pronoun = "**her hand**." This genitive is also partitive, because Jesus grasps only a part of her, namely her hand (Smyth, 1341; Wallace 84–86).

καὶ ἀφῆκεν αὐτὴν ὁ πυρετός.

- καί coor. conj. (paratactic, connects this sentence to the previous one) = "**and**."
- ὁ πυρετός nom. sing. masc. of the noun ὁ πυρετός (subject) = "**the fever**."
- ἀφῆκεν aor. act. ind. 3rd pers. sing. of the verb ἀφίημι (punctiliar aorist) = "**left**" (her). The verb ἀφίημι is also used in Mark to depict the departure of demons/unclean spirits from a possessed person. Compare how the leprosy "left" in 1:42.
- αὐτήν acc. sing. fem. of the 3rd person personal pronoun αὐτός, -ή, -ό (direct object) = "**her**" (Simon's mother-in-law).

καὶ διηκόνει αὐτοῖς

- καί coor. conj. (paratactic, connects this sentence to the previous one) = "**and**."
- διηκόνει impf. act. ind. 3rd pers. sing. of the verb διακονέω (inceptive imperfect expressing the onset of an action that will continue) = "**she began serving**." Note that a thematic interpretation of the healed person's serving (a meal) may suggest that the role of healthy people in general is to serve. This role anticipates the role Jesus sees for himself (10:45), his disciples (9:9:35; 10:43) and all who would follow him (9:35)—a role associated in the ancient world with women and slaves.
- αὐτοῖς dat. plur. masc. of the 3rd person personal pronoun αὐτός, -ή, -ό (dative instead of accusative as the direct object after certain verbs of "serving") = "**them**." The antecedent of αὐτοῖς is Jesus and the four disciples with whom he entered the house.

<1:32>'Οψίας δὲ γενομένης, ὅτε ἔδυ ὁ ἥλιος, ἔφερον πρὸς αὐτὸν πάντας τοὺς κακῶς ἔχοντας καὶ τοὺς δαιμονιζομένους· = **Now when evening came, after the sun set, they (people) brought to him all the ones who were ill and the demon-possessed.**

'Οψίας δὲ γενομένης, ὅτε ἔδυ ὁ ἥλιος,

- δέ postpositive coord. conj. (paratactic, connects this sentence to the previous one and suggests the introduction of new information) = "**And**" "**Now**" (Decker 33). Given the context, the conjunction here has no adversative force.

- 'Οψίας (anarthrous) gen. sing. fem of the noun ἡ ὀψία (subject of the genitive absolute circumstantial clause) = "**evening**." This is a general term for evening.

- γενομένης, aor. mid. (in form) participle gen. sing. fem. of the verb γίνομαι (a temporal circumstantial participle that is a genitive absolute, in the aorist expressing time previous to the time of the main verb) = "**being evening**" or "**when it was evening**" or "**after evening came**" or simply "**that evening**" (Williams 39). For the designation of this verb as deponent, see the comments on Mark 1:4.

Together these two words constitute a genitive absolute use of the participle, the combination of a participle and a noun in the genitive, the noun serving as the subject of the action expressed by the participle. The construction in the genitive signals that the participle is grammatically independent (absolute) of any nouns in the sentence and therefore stands alone as an aorist circumstantial clause (expressing time previous to the action of the main verb).

- ὅτε subord. conj. (temporal, followed by an indicative) = "**when.**"
- ὁ ἥλιος nom. sing. masc. of the noun ὁ ἥλιος (subject of the verb ἔδυ) = "**the sun.**"
- ἔδυ aor. act. ind. 3rd pers. sing. of the verb δύνω (punctiliar aorist) = "**went down**" or "**set.**" The whole phrase means, "**when the sun had set**" or "**at sundown**" or "**after the sun set.**"

This whole temporal clause is a Markan two-step progression. The first phrase gives a general temporal reference ("when it was evening"), and this is followed by a second phrase that specifies a more precise time ("when the sun set"). In Mark's depiction, sunset was the time when evening began and the Sabbath ended shortly thereafter and people were permitted to travel and work again. As soon as they were allowed by law to travel again, they carried the sick to Jesus. And Jesus was legally free to heal.

ἔφερον πρὸς αὐτὸν πάντας τοὺς κακῶς ἔχοντας καὶ τοὺς δαιμονιζομένους·

- ἔφερον impf. act. ind. 3rd pers. plur. of the verb φέρω (imperfect of repeated action, depicting a continuous process) = **"they (people) were bringing"** or **"they kept bringing."** Note the unspecified subject ("they" = the whole city [vs. 33]). The imperfect tense gives emphasis to the repeated actions of a parade of people bringing the sick and possessed to Jesus.

- πρὸς αὐτόν prepositional phrase (expressing motion toward) with πρός + the accusative, here acc. sing. masc. of the 3rd person personal pronoun αὐτός, -ή, -ό (object of the preposition) = **"to him"** (Jesus). The phrase is translated just like an indirect object (αὐτῷ) in the dative would be translated, but in a way that emphasizes the movement implied in the verb.

- πάντας acc. plur. masc. of the pronominal adjective πᾶς, πᾶσα, πᾶν (modifying the following substantive participle in the predicate position) = **"all"** [individually] or **"everyone."**

- τοὺς κακῶς ἔχοντας is an expression literally meaning **"the ones who have (it) badly."** Idiomatically, it means **"those who are ill"** (Decker 33; Williams 39). Τοὺς ἔχοντας is pres. act. participle acc. plur. masc. of the verb ἔχω (substantive use of the participle/direct object of ἔφερον) = **"those who are sick."** The participle in the present expresses an action or state concurrent with the action of the main verb. As part verb, the participle is modified by an adverb κακῶς (note the -ως suffix as one of the signs of an adverb). As part adjective, the participle here functions substantively as a noun and is modified by the pronominal adjective πάντας = **all those [individually] who were sick.** The participle in the present depicts the ongoing state of illness. The verb ἔχω + an adverb is a periphrasis for (and therefore equivalent to) the verb εἰμί + an adjective (Smyth 1438).

- καί coor. conj. (simple connective, connecting two direct objects of ἔφερον, both of which are substantive participles) = **"and."**

- τοὺς δαιμονιζομένους pres. pass. participle acc. plur. masc. of the verb δαιμονίζω (substantive participle/second part of a compound direct object) = "**the demon-possessed**" or "**those who were possessed by demons.**" The participle in the present depicts the ongoing condition of possession.

Note that these two groups of people (the sick and the possessed) parallel in reverse order the recipients of Jesus' actions in the previous two stories (an exorcism and a healing). We may infer from Mark's parallelism that the word had spread about these two events and that people have therefore brought others who would benefit from the same actions on the part of Jesus.

<1:33> καὶ ἦν ὅλη ἡ πόλις ἐπισυνηγμένη πρὸς τὴν θύραν. = **And the whole city was gathered at the door.**

καὶ ... ὅλη ἡ πόλις

- καί coord. conj. (paratactic, connects this sentence to the previous one) = "**and.**"
- ὅλη nom. sing. fem. of the pronominal adjective ὅλος, -η, -ον (modifies the noun in a predicate position) = "**the city as a whole**" or "**the entire city.**"
- ἡ πόλις nom. sing. fem. of the noun ἡ πόλις (subject) = "**the [entire] city**" (of Capernaum).

ἦν ... ἐπισυνηγμένη πρὸς τὴν θύραν

- ἦν ... ἐπισυνηγμένη impf. act. ind. 3rd pers. sing. of the equative verb εἰμί + the perf. mid. or pass. participle nom. sing. fem. of the verb ἐπισυνάγω, agreeing with ἡ πόλις (a periphrastic use of the participle that combines the verb εἰμί with a perfect participle to express the perfect—compare English "was gathered") = "**was gathered**" or, put affirmatively, "**gathered.**" The periphrastic use of the verb (εἰμί + the participle) emphasizes state rather than action (Smyth 599a).
- πρὸς τὴν θύραν prepositional phrase (expressing motion toward and arrival at) with πρός + the accusative, here the acc. sing. fem. of the noun ἡ θύρα = "**toward the door**" or, since the verb also expresses motion toward, the preposition presents the place of arrival, "**at the**

door." Perhaps the prepositional phrase conveys the sense of "facing the door" or pressing in to get to the door.

<1:34> καὶ ἐθεράπευσεν πολλοὺς κακῶς ἔχοντας ποικίλαις νόσοις καὶ δαιμόνια πολλὰ ἐξέβαλεν καὶ οὐκ ἤφιεν λαλεῖν τὰ δαιμόνια, ὅτι ᾔδεισαν αὐτόν. = **and he healed many who were sick with various illnesses and he drove out many demons, and he would not permit the demons to speak, because they knew him.**

καὶ ἐθεράπευσεν πολλοὺς κακῶς ἔχοντας ποικίλαις νόσοις

- καί coor. conj. (paratactic, connects this sentence to the previous one) = "**and**."

- ἐθεράπευσεν aor. act. ind. 3rd pers. sing. of the verb θεραπεύω (a global aorist encompassing the many acts of healing) = "**he (Jesus) healed**" or "**he cured.**"

- πολλούς acc. plur. masc. of the adjective πολύς, πολή, πολύ (substantive/direct object) = "**many.**" This adjective is used substantively without the article (BDAG, πολύς 2.a). The grammar does not mean that Jesus healed "many" of those brought to him, but that those brought to him and whom he healed were "many" (Williams 39–40). Matthew 8:16 avoids this potential confusion by stating that Jesus healed "all."

- κακῶς ἔχοντας pres. act. participle acc. plur. masc. of the verb ἔχω, agreeing with πολλούς (a circumstantial participle expressing time contemporaneous with the time of the main verb or an attributive participle modifying the anarthrous substantive πολλούς). Combined with the abverb κακῶς, the two words form an idiom meaning "**who were sick.**" The verb ἔχω + an adverb is a periphrasis for (and therefore equivalent to) the verb εἰμί + an adjective (Smyth 1438). If ἔχοντας is a circumstantial participle, it may be causal (Smyth 2064; Wallace 631–33) = "**he healed many because they had various illnesses.**"

- ποικίλαις νόσοις dat. plur. fem. of the noun ἡ νόσος ("illness") modified by the dat. plur. fem. of the adjective ποικίλος, -η, ον (dative of manner explaining *how* they were sick) = "**with various illnesses.**" Νόσοις should not be translated "diseases" as there was no concept of disease (understood as foreign microbes in the body) in the first century.

A LINGUISTIC MODEL TO ANALYZE NEW TESTAMENT GREEK

καὶ δαιμόνια πολλὰ ἐξέβαλεν

- καί coor. conj. (paratactic, connects this sentence to the previous one) = "**and**."
- ἐξέβαλεν aor. act. ind. 3rd pers. sing. of the verb ἐκβάλλω (a global aorist expressing many acts of exorcism as one act) = "**he (Jesus) drove out**" or "**he exorcized**" or "**he cast out**."
- δαιμόνια πολλά acc. plur. neut. of the noun τὸ δαιμόνιον modified by the acc. plur. neut. of the adjective πολύς, πολλά, πολύ (direct object) = "**many demons**." Note that the ending -ιον suggests that the word is a diminutive, i. e. these evil spirits were "little demons." Again, the reference to "many" does not mean that Jesus healed only many of those brought to him, but that those brought to him and whom he healed were many.

Putting the direct object first gives it emphasis and also creates a chiastic pattern with the previous clause = verb/noun : noun/verb = he healed/many sick : demons/ he drove out. Also the two acts of Jesus parallel the two groups brought to him: they brought the sick and the demon-possessed, and he healed the sick and exorcized the demons. The two global aorists depict all of Jesus' responses to the presentation of many human needs.

Note that Mark is now using the term "demons" rather than "unclean spirits." Probably the phrase "unclean spirits" is simply another Markan term for demons, although an "unclean spirit" may be one type of demon, just as the "mute and deaf spirit" may be a particular kind of demon (9:25). At the same time, the choice to refer to them as unclean spirits rather than as demons serves the Markan motif of "purity and defilement."

καὶ οὐκ ἤφιεν λαλεῖν τὰ δαιμόνια,

- καί coor. conj. (paratactic, connects this sentence to the previous one) = "**and**." May imply "**but**."
- οὐκ adverbial negative (modifying the main verb, used [usually with the indicative] to negate a fact) = "**not**." Note how οὐ ends with a kappa, because the following word begins with a vowel with soft breathing.
- ἤφιεν impf. act. ind. 3rd pers. sing of the verb ἀφίημι (imperfect of repeated or customary action in the past) = "**he (Jesus) was not allowing**" or "**he would not let**" or "**would not permit**."

- λαλεῖν pres. act. infinitive of the verb λαλέω (complementary infinitive after verbs of permission, expressing repeated action by means of the present tense) = "**to speak**" or simply "**speak.**"
- **τὰ δαιμόνια** acc. plur. neut. of the noun τὸ δαιμόνιον (subject of the infinitive) = "**he would not permit the demons to speak.**" Because infinitives are verbal nouns, they can take subjects and objects. The subject of an infinitive is in the nominative case when it is the same as the subject of the main verb. When the subject of the infinitive is also the direct object (as it is here) of the main verb (ἤφιεν), then the subject of the infinitive is in the accusative case (Smyth 1973; Wallace 192–93). The context makes it clear that τὰ δαιμόνια is the subject of the infinitive and the object of the main verb ἤφιεν (since it is clearly the demons who would speak, if Jesus had allowed them to do so). This prohibition is clearly linked to the outburst of the unclean spirit earlier in Capernaum when he told the unclean spirit to "be quiet" because they blurted out his identity as "the Holy One of God" (1:24–25).

ὅτι ᾔδεισαν αὐτόν.

- ὅτι subord. conj. (causal, introducing a dependent clause) = "**because.**"
- ᾔδεισαν pluperf. (imperfect in meaning) act. ind. 3rd pers. plur. of the verb οἶδα (an unusual pluperfect form that functions as an imperfect, here an imperfect expressing an ongoing condition) = "**they (the demons) knew him.**" On the other hand, the imperfect may express a simple action in the past (Wallace 586) = "**they recognized him.**"
- αὐτόν acc. sing. masc. of the 3rd pers. personal pronoun αὐτός, -ή, -ό (direct object) = "**him**" (Jesus).

This situation is part of the messianic secret in Mark where the demons know who Jesus is, while no one else does. Here Jesus is working to keep his identity as the son of God from becoming public. Clearly, those present ignore what the demons say, thus preserving the secrecy, for now. If the word gets out, Jesus will be in grave legal trouble, as it was this identity that later led to his conviction by the High Priests and his subsequent execution by the Romans (14:61–64).

<1:35> Καὶ πρωῒ ἔννυχα λίαν ἀναστὰς ἐξῆλθεν καὶ ἀπῆλθεν εἰς ἔρημον τόπον κἀκεῖ προσηύχετο = **and very early (in the morning), while still quite**

dark, after arising, he came out and he went off to a desert place and there he was praying.

Καὶ πρωΐ ἔννυχα λίαν ἀναστὰς ἐξῆλθεν

- καί coor. conj. (paratactic, connects this sentence to the previous one) = "**and**" or it introduces new information = "**now**."
- πρωΐ adverb modifying ἐξῆλθεν (temporal, expressing *when* Jesus came out) = "**early**" or "**early in the morning**" or "**in the morning watch**." Πρωΐ refers to the last watch of the night that extended from about three o'clock to six o'clock.
- ἔννυχα acc. plur. neut. of the adjective ἔννυχος, -η, -ον (neuter singular adjective used here as a temporal adverb modifying ἐξῆλθεν and expressing *when* Jesus came out) = "**at night-time**" or "**while still dark**" or "**by night**" (Decker 35).
- λίαν adverb (modifying the adverb ἔννυχα) = "**very**." [λίαν may modify πρωΐ] Together the adverbs mean, "**early in the morning, while (still) quite dark**" or "**early morning, while still night**."

This is a typical Markan two-step progression in which the first step names a general period (the last watch of the night from three to six) and the second step specifies the darkness (typical of the earlier part of this watch). Together the three adverbs emphasize the early hour of Jesus' activity. Almost everyone was up and about in the morning watch, which ended at sunrise, and the time started being marked by hours on a sun dial. Since the workday began at sunrise, workers were expected to be at work by then. Jesus arose much earlier than everyone else, since he ventured out while it was still dark.

- ἀναστάς aor. act. participle nom. sing. masc. of the verb ἀνίστημι, agreeing with the subject of the main verb, "he" (Jesus) (temporal circumstantial participle, which, in the aorist, expresses time previous to the time of the main verb) = "**after arising**" or simply "**rising**" or "**after he arose**" or (paralleling the main verb) "**he arose and went out**." Obviously, the participle refers to "getting up in the morning."
- ἐξῆλθεν 2nd aor. act. ind. 3rd person sing. of the verb ἐξέρχομαι (punctiliar aorist) = "**he came out**" or "**went out**." For the designation of the

present tense but not the aorist tense of this verb as a deponent, see the comments on Mark 1:7, 9.

καὶ ἀπῆλθεν εἰς ἔρημον τόπον

- καί coord. conj. (paratactic, connects this sentence to the previous one) = "**and.**"
- ἀπῆλθεν aor. act. ind. 3rd person sing. of the deponent verb ἀπέρχομαι (punctiliar aorist) = "**he went off**" or "**he went away**" or "**he departed.**"
- εἰς ἔρημον τόπον prepositional phrase (expressing motion toward or into) with εἰς + the accusative, here acc. sing. masc. of the noun ὁ τόπος and modified by the acc. sing. masc. of the adjective ἔρημος, -η, -ον = "**into a desert place**" or, better, "**to a deserted place**" or "**to an isolated spot.**"

Note the contrast between the village where people give Jesus honor ("everyone's seeking you") and the deserted place where Jesus is alone in prayer with God. The source of Jesus' authority and activity come from what God wants and not from what people want. The contrast between what humans want and what God wills is the first expression of this important Markan theme. The deserted place recalls John's preparation in the desert (1:3–4) and Jesus' confirmation from God (1:11) and his defeat of Satan in the desert (1:12).

κἀκεῖ προσηύχετο

- κἀκεῖ contraction of the coord. conj. καί and the adverb ἐκεῖ (adverb of place designating where Jesus was praying) = "**and there.**" Κἀκεῖ is formed when καί and ἐκεῖ unite by crasis. "Crasis is the contraction of a vowel . . . at the end of a word with a vowel or diphthong beginning the following word" (Smyth 62). In crasis, a diphthong often loses its final vowel (Smyth 67). Hence the iota of the καί is dropped. Dropping the iota juxtaposes the alpha and the epsilon, and these vowels contract to a long alpha (Smyth 66, cf. 59). A coronis (written in English as an apostrophe) is placed "over the syllable resulting from the contraction" (Smyth 62).
- προσηύχετο impf. mid. (in form) ind. 3rd pers. sing. of the deponent verb προσεύχομαι (imperfect of continuous action) = "**he (Jesus) was praying.**" Perhaps the imperfect is ingressive = "**he started praying.**"

Prayer is an important activity in Mark. On the one hand, it is the means by which one strengthens faith and gains access to God's power for healing and exorcism (e.g. 9:29, 11:24). On the other hand, as here, it seems to function as the means by which Jesus reorients or remains oriented to his mission as agent of God's rule.

<1:36> καὶ κατεδίωξεν αὐτὸν Σίμων καὶ οἱ μετ' αὐτοῦ, καὶ εὗρον αὐτὸν = **and Simon and those with him tracked him down and found him.**

καὶ κατεδίωξεν αὐτὸν Σίμων καὶ οἱ μετ' αὐτοῦ,

- Καί coor. conj. (paratactic, connects this sentence to the previous one) = "**and.**"
- κατεδίωξεν aor. act. ind. 3rd pers. sing. of the verb καταδιώκω (punctiliar aorist) = "**and (he) pursued him**" or "**hunted him down**" or "**tracked him down.**" The prefix κατα- is an intensifier for the meaning of the root word, such that the simple verb "pursue" is strengthened to mean "track down" or "pursue closely" (Decker 35). Σίμων is the singular subject of the singular verb, even though the whole subject is a compound (Williams 40).
- αὐτόν acc. sing. masc. of the 3rd person personal pronoun αὐτός, ἡ, -ό (direct object) = "**him**" (Jesus).
- Σίμων nom. sing. masc. of the proper name Σίμων (first part of the compound subject) = "**Simon.**" Σίμων καὶ οἱ μετ' αὐτου is the compound subject of the sentence.
- καί coor. conj. (simple connective, joining two parts of a compound subject) = "**and.**"
- οἱ μετ' αὐτοῦ prepositional phrase with an article, functioning together with the article as a substantive (Williams 40). Μετ' αὐτοῦ is a prepositional phrase with the genitive, here the gen. sing. masc. of the 3rd person pronoun (the alpha of the μετά is elided when it is followed by a word that begins with alpha and has soft breathing) = "**with him**" (Simon). The article οἱ makes the substantive phrase a nom. plur. masc. (subject) = "**the ones with him**" or "**those with him.**" The phrase "those with him" may refer to Andrew, James, and John (1:29). The naming of Simon among other unnamed persons places him in a position of leadership.

καὶ εὗρον αὐτὸν

- καί coor. conj. (simple connective, joining two independent clauses) = "**and**."
- εὗρον 2nd aor. act. ind. 3rd pers. plur. of the verb εὑρίσκω (punctiliar aorist) = "**they found**."
- αὐτόν acc. sing. masc. of the 3rd pers. personal pronoun αὐτός, -ή, -ό (direct object) = "**him**" (Jesus).

<1:37> καὶ λέγουσιν αὐτῷ ὅτι πάντες ζητοῦσίν σε. = **and they say to him, [that] "All are seeking you."**

καὶ λέγουσιν αὐτῷ

- καί coord. conj. (paratactic, connects this sentence with the previous one) = "**and**."
- λέγουσιν pres. act. ind. 3rd pers. plur. of the verb λέγω (historical present) = "**they say**" or "**they said**."
- αὐτῷ dat. sing. masc. of the 3rd person personal pronoun αὐτός, -ή, -ό (indirect object) = "**to him**" (Jesus).

ὅτι Πάντες ζητοῦσίν σε.

- ὅτι subord. conj. (introducing direct speech, called a "recitative" ὅτι, to be translated as a comma and quotation marks) = "**, ...**"
- Πάντες nom. plur. masc. of the pronoun πάς, πάσα, πάν (subject) = "**all**." The plural of πάς means "all" [individually], whereas in the singular it means "everyone."
- ζητοῦσίν pres. act. ind. 3rd pers. plur. of the verb ζητέω (descriptive present depicting action in progress at the time of speaking—Wallace 518) = "**are seeking**" or "**are looking for**."
- σε acc. sing. masc. of the 2nd person personal pronoun σύ (direct object) = "**you**" (Jesus). Note that the two accents on the word preceding this (ζητοῦσίν) provide the accent for the enclitic σε.

Simon seems to be enamored with the public attention Jesus is getting for his healing. In Mark's carefully developed narrative, this is perhaps the first sign of misunderstanding by the disciples. Their misunderstanding arises here from their desire to gain public honor from their association with Jesus and their assumption that Jesus too will be enamored by this public honor. Jesus will have none of it, because he gets his orientation from God (in prayer) and not from people.

<1:38> καὶ λέγει αὐτοῖς, Ἄγωμεν ἀλλαχοῦ εἰς τὰς ἐχομένας κωμοπόλεις, ἵνα καὶ ἐκεῖ κηρύξω, εἰς τοῦτο γὰρ ἐξῆλθον = **and he says to them, "Let's go elsewhere, to the neighboring towns, in order that also there I might proclaim, for on account of that I came out."**

καὶ λέγει αὐτοῖς,

- καί coor. conj. (paratactic, connects this sentence to the previous one) = **"and."**
- λέγει pres. act. ind. 3rd pers. sing. of the verb λέγω (historical present) = **"he (Jesus) says"** or **"he said."**
- αὐτοῖς dat. plur. masc. of the 3rd person personal pronoun αὐτός, ή, ὁ (indirect object) = **"he (Jesus) says to them."** What follows in direct speech is the direct object of the verb λέγει.

Ἄγωμεν ἀλλαχοῦ εἰς τὰς ἐχομένας κωμοπόλεις,

- Ἄγωμεν pres. act. subj. 1st person plur. of the verb ἄγω (hortatory subjunctive) = **"Let's (Let us) go."** Exhortation in the subjunctive is more of a command than a request or an invitation.
- ἀλλαχοῦ adverb (place, modifying the verb ἄγωμεν and answering the question "where") = **"elsewhere."**
- εἰς τὰς ἐχομένας κωμοπόλεις prepositional phrase (expressing motion toward or into) with εἰς + the accusative, here the acc. plur. fem. of the noun ἡ κωμοπόλις = **"into the village-cities"** or **"to the towns."** In Mark's narrative, Jesus does not go into the major cities of Galilee.
- ἐχομένας pres. mid. participle acc. plur. fem. of the verb ἔχω modifying τὰς. . . κωμοπόλεις in the attributive position (attributive participle, expressing spatial proximity) = **"next"** or **"adjoining"** or **"neighboring"** (Decker 37; Williams 41). Jesus has a mission for the rule of God to reach many villages in Galilee (compare 1:14).

ἵνα καὶ ἐκεῖ κηρύξω

- ἵνα subord. conj. (introducing a dependent clause of purpose, with a subjunctive) = **"in order that."**
- καί adverb (καί of balanced contrast [Smyth 2885–87; Wallace 671], modifying the verb κηρύξω) = **"as well"** or **"also."**
- ἐκεῖ adverb (place) = **"there."**
- κηρύξω aor. act. subj. 1st pers. sing. of the verb κηρύσσω (subjunctive in a purpose clause with ἵνα) = **"I (Jesus) might proclaim."** Although the subjunctive is in the aorist (suggesting a single action), the meaning is like a global aorist (encompassing repeated future acts of proclaiming). In Mark, the word κηρύσσω refers primarily to the proclamation of the rule of God and the actions attendant on its arrival.

εἰς τοῦτο γὰρ ἐξῆλθον

- γάρ postpositive subord. conj. (explanatory, introducing an explanatory clause) = **"for"** (Decker 37).
- εἰς τοῦτο prepositional phrase (expressing purpose) with εἰς + the accusative, here the acc. sing. neut. of the demonstrative pronoun οὗτος, αὕτη, τοῦτο. The εἰς here has the metaphorical meaning of movement toward a goal = **"for this"** or **"for this purpose"** or **"on account of this"** or even **"that's why."** The antecedent of τοῦτο is the whole ἵνα clause.
- ἐξῆλθον 2nd aor. act. ind. 3rd person sing. of the verb ἐξέρχομαι (punctiliar aorist, expressing the act of coming out to proclaim or the whole process of emerging as a public figure) = **"I came out."** For the designation of the present tense but not the aorist tense of this verb as a deponent, see the comments on Mark 1:7, 9.

Note the double entendre of the phrase "why I came out" (Decker 37). In the immediate sense, it explains why he came out from the house that morning to pray. Yet in his use of it here, "why I came out" also refers to his sense of vocation as agent of the rule of God, namely, that he is anointed to proclaim the rule of God widely in Israel—here expressed as going "on to the next towns so I might proclaim there also." The word ἔρχομαι is used several times in Mark to refer to Jesus' vocation (e. g. 2:17). Also, in this regard, one imagines Mark's narrative may be portraying Jesus in prayer as a means to resist the temptation to stay in Capernaum in order to enjoy the honor granted him in this one place and instead to remain faithful in his vocation to proclaim throughout Galilee.

<1:39> καὶ ἦλθεν κηρύσσων εἰς τὰς συναγωγὰς αὐτῶν εἰς ὅλην τὴν Γαλιλαίαν καὶ τὰ δαιμόνια ἐκβάλλων = **and he went proclaiming in their synagogues in all Galilee and driving out the demons.**

καὶ ἦλθεν κηρύσσων εἰς τὰς συναγωγὰς αὐτῶν εἰς ὅλην τὴν Γαλιλαίαν

- καί coor. conj. (paratactic, connects this sentence to the previous one) = "**and**." In context, the actions depicted in this sentence follow logically from Jesus' words in the previous sentence, i. e. as the outcome. As such, καί may perhaps be translated accordingly = "**so**" or "**and so**."

- ἦλθεν 2nd aor. act. ind. 3rd pers. sing. of the verb ἔρχομαι (punctiliar aorist) = "**he came**" or "**he went**." Note that ἔρχομαι can mean either "came" or "went." When the word is translated in different ways in English, we therefore miss the thematic repetition of this word. So, Jesus *came out* of the synagogue and *went* into the house (1:29); he *came out* of the house and *went* to a deserted place (1:35); and he said he would *go out* to go to the next towns; and so he *went* everywhere in Galilee—all translating the same root word. The two participles that follow (κηρύσσων and ἐκβάλλων) express the manner in which Jesus went throughout Galilee. For the designation of the present tense but not the aorist tense of this verb as a deponent, see the comments on Mark 1:7, 9.

- κηρύσσων pres. act. participle nom. sing. masc. of the verb κηρύσσω, agreeing with the subject of the sentence "he" (Jesus) (circumstantial participle that explains the "manner" in which Jesus went) = "**proclaiming**." So Jesus did what he said he would do.

- εἰς τὰς συναγωγάς prepositional phrase (expressing motion toward or into) with εἰς + the accusative, here the acc. plur. fem. of the noun ἡ συναγωγή = "**into the synagogues**." Εἰς may be a substitute for ἐν = "**in their synagogues**."

- αὐτῶν gen. plur. masc. of the 3rd person personal pronoun αὐτός, -ή, -ό (genitive of possession referring to the people in the neighboring villages of Galilee—Bratcher 64) = "**in(to) their synagogues**." Note how, at the beginning of Mark's story, Jesus proclaims in synagogues, whereas later he will go mostly to houses or stay out in open/deserted places.

- εἰς ὅλην τὴν Γαλιλαίαν prepositional phrase (expressing motion toward or into) with εἰς + the accusative, here the acc. sing. fem. of the noun Γαλιλαία, modified in the predicate position by the acc. sing. fem. of the pronominal adjective ὅλος, -η, -ον (object of the preposition) = "**into Galilee as a whole**" or "**in(to) all Galilee.**" One would have expected the preposition ἐν ("in") here. Either εἰς means "in" or it stands in apposition to the first prepositional phrase (εἰς τὰς συναγωγάς). In either case, these two prepositional phrases could modify ἦλθεν ("he went into") rather than κηρύσσων ("he proclaimed into"), although the first prepositional phrase may modify κηρύσσων and the second ἦλθεν (Decker 37); or both could modify κηρύσσω. In the previous verse, we get the impression Jesus is going only to the villages near Capernaum ("the neighboring villages"). Now, we see that Galilee as a whole is the larger arena of Jesus' proclaiming, at least at this early stage of his activity (compare 1:14).

The position of these prepositional phrases indicates that they modify two participles, both the one that precedes them (κηρύσσων) and the one that follows them (ἐκβάλλων). The structural pattern is this: (1) participle; (2) open slot; (3) καί; (4) participle. Whatever is placed in the open slot of this structure modifies both participles. Thus, Jesus' preaching and his casting out of demons occurred "in their synagogues in Galilee as a whole."

καὶ τὰ δαιμόνια ἐκβάλλων

- καί coor. conj. (simple connective, joining the two circumstantial participles that modify the main verb) = "**and.**"
- ἐκβάλλων pres. act. participle nom. sing. masc. of the verb ἐκβάλλω, agreeing with the subject of the main verb "he" (Jesus) (a temporal circumstantial participle of manner expressing "how" Jesus came/parallels κηρύσσων) = "**driving out.**"
- τὰ δαιμόνια acc. plur. neut. of the noun τὸ δαιμόνιον (direct object of the participle) = "**the demons.**" In this summary of much activity, the double participles ("proclaiming" and "driving out") clarify how typically Jesus' proclaiming of the rule of God was accompanied by works of power over the demons.

WHAT FOLLOWS

At the end of this episode, we are left with a picture of Jesus' traveling from village to village. The next episode reinforces the idea that the growing popularity of Jesus in Capernaum will be repeated in other places; and so in Jesus' travels, he cleanses a leper in what appears to be a private healing (1:40–45). Although Jesus tells the cleansed leper to be quiet, he nevertheless spreads the word widely, with the result that the crowds who gather around Jesus are so large that Jesus can no longer enter into a city. He has to stay outside the villages in deserted places. Yet, people come to him from everywhere, and when he returns to his house in Capernaum after a few days, so many people gather that there is not even room at the door (2:1–12). After establishing this ongoing pattern of growing popular support, the Markan narrator then introduces a different response to Jesus' activity, namely, opposition by the authorities (2:6–7).

6

Jesus and the Leper
Mark 1:40–45

PREVIEW

The Markan narrative has been presenting episodes that display, on the one hand, the activity of the rule of God and, on the other hand, the human response of faith: the call of the disciples, the exorcism at Capernaum, the healing of Peter's mother-in-law, and a summary of other exorcisms and healings. This episode presents a new dimension of the activity of the rule of God—power over the forces of impurity—and presents a new trait of the response of faith—persistence in the face of an obstacle. A leper approaches Jesus with the determination to overcome Jesus' potential resistance to touching a leper (persistence in faith), and Jesus "cleanses" the man of the leprosy (the rule of God overcomes impurity). Mark also tells stories to display the consequences of Jesus' activity—either support by the people or conflict with authorities. In this episode, the response by the people is so great that Jesus has to stay out in deserted areas because the huge crowds prevent him from being able to enter villages.

‹1:40› Καὶ ἔρχεται πρὸς αὐτὸν λεπρὸς   And (there) comes to him a leper
    παρακαλῶν αὐτὸν   begging him
[καὶ γονυπετῶν]   [and kneeling]

καὶ λέγων αὐτῷ	and saying to him
ὅτι Ἐὰν <u>θέλῃς</u>	that "If you <u>want</u> (to),
<u>δύνασαί</u> με <u>καθαρίσαι</u>.	you are <u>able</u> to <u>cleanse</u> me."
‹1:41› καὶ σπλαγχνισθεὶς	And being moved by compassion,
ἐκτείνας τὴν χεῖρα αὐτοῦ	after stretching out his hand,
ἥψατο	he touched (him)
καὶ λέγει αὐτῷ,	and (he) says to him
<u>Θέλω</u>,	"I <u>want</u> (to).
<u>καθαρίσθητι</u>·	Be <u>cleansed</u>."
‹1:42› καὶ <u>εὐθὺς</u> ἀπῆλθεν ἀπ' αὐτοῦ <u>ἡ λέπρα</u>,	And <u>immediately</u> the <u>leprosy</u> went from him,
καὶ <u>ἐκαθαρίσθη</u>.	and he was <u>cleansed</u>.
‹1:43› καὶ ἐμβριμησάμενος αὐτῷ	And upbraiding him
<u>εὐθὺς</u> ἐξέβαλεν αὐτόν	<u>immediately</u> he drove him out
‹1:44› καὶ λέγει αὐτῷ,	and (he) says to him,
Ὅρα μηδενὶ μηδὲν εἴπῃς,	"See (that) you say nothing to anyone,
ἀλλὰ ὕπαγε σεαυτὸν δεῖξον τῷ ἱερεῖ	but go show yourself to the priest
καὶ προσένεγκε περὶ τοῦ <u>καθαρισμοῦ</u> σου	and offer for your <u>cleansing</u>
ἃ προσέταξεν Μωϋσῆς,	what things Moses commanded
εἰς μαρτύριον αὐτοῖς.	as a witness to them.
‹1:45› ὁ δὲ <u>ἐξελθὼν</u>	But after <u>going out</u>
ἤρξατο κηρύσσειν πολλὰ	he began to proclaim freely
καὶ διαφημίζειν τὸν λόγον,	and to spread the word
ὥστε μηκέτι αὐτὸν <u>δύνασθαι</u>	with the result that no longer was he [Jesus] <u>able</u>
φανερῶς εἰς πόλιν <u>εἰσελθεῖν</u>,	openly <u>to enter into</u> a city
ἀλλ' ἔξω ἐπ' ἐρήμοις τόποις ἦν·	but was outside, in deserted places.
καὶ <u>ἤρχοντο πρὸς αὐτὸν</u> πάντοθεν.	and they (people) were <u>coming to him</u> from everywhere.

MARKAN WORD FIELDS AND MOTIFS

There are three word fields in this episode. (1) Regarding the cleansing of the leper, the focus of the episode is on the word field of "purity and defilement." (2) Integral to the relation between the leper and Jesus is the word field of "God's will and human faith." (3) Finally, the motif of "hiddenness and openness" plays a role in this episode. All three of these word fields are embedded in the larger word field of "the rule of God."

"Purity and Defilement"

Because the "healing" of the leper is presented as a "cleansing," therefore "purity and defilement" is the primary word field of this episode: "leper" (λέπρος), "leprosy," (ἡ λέπρα), "cleanse" (καθαρίζω—3 times), "cleansing" (τοῦ καθαρισμοῦ), and the ritual of being declared clean by showing oneself "to the priest" (τῷ ἱερεῖ) and by "offering the sacrifice" (προσένεγκε) that Moses commanded (προσέταξεν Μωϋσῆς). In Mark, purity language has already been introduced with Jesus' baptism "by the *holy* spirit" (ἐν πνεύματι ἁγίῳ—1:8, 10) and with the identification of Jesus by the demon as "the *holy one* of God" (ὁ ἅγιος τοῦ θεοῦ—1:24). Defilement language has already been introduced with reference to a man possessed by an "*unclean* spirit" (ἐν πνεύματι ἀκαθάρτῳ—1:23).

In Mark, the powerful presence of the rule of God overcomes the power of defilement. Ordinarily, people would withdraw from the pernicious influence of impure people and things. They would protect their holiness by separating from defilement. With the arrival of the rule of God, this process is reversed. Jesus touched (ἥψατο) the leper, and, instead of Jesus' being defiled, the leper was cleansed (ἐκαθαρίσθη). The "holy one" spreads holiness and wholeness to push back the boundaries of impurity. The rule of God invades the territory of uncleanness to overcome it with holiness. In Mark, purity and defilement issues appear again in episodes about eating with sinners (2:15-17), defiling the Sabbath (2:23—3:6), unclean spirits entering pigs in a graveyard in gentile territory (5:1-20), a woman with a flow of blood (5:25-34), a dead child (5:35-43), impure food (7:1-23), and gentiles eating bread in the desert (8:1-10), among others. In each case, the holy power of the rule of God prevails.

Note the irony that Jesus and the leper have traded places. At the opening, the leper was excluded from cities because of uncleanness while

Jesus was moving about freely. At the end, the leper goes out and spreads the word freely while Jesus is prevented from entering villages (either because of his popularity or because he is now considered unclean) and must stay in deserted places.

"God's Will and Human Faith"

A second word field focuses on language about the will of God. The leper challenges Jesus with the words "If you want/will" (Ἐὰν θέλῃς) and the affirmation that "you are able" (δύνασαι). In response, Jesus is "moved by compassion" (σπλαγχνισθείς) and declares that "I do want/will" (θέλω). The result of the healing is that "immediately the leprosy left him" (εὐθὺς ἀπῆλθεν ἀπ' αὐτοῦ ἡ λέπρα). The language here reflects human faith in God's will, in particular the faith of the suppliant expressed in action and words: "he came to Jesus" (ἔρχεται πρὸς αὐτόν); he was "pleading" (παρακαλῶν), and "kneeling," (γονυπετῶν); and he "spoke" (λέγων) the request. In so doing, he sought to overcome the obstacle to his cleansing—Jesus' possible resistance to touching him.

God's power and human faith are the larger narrative contexts in which the cleansing of leprosy is but one example. God's power is now present to rule over non-human forces that oppress, destroy, and diminish human life. As an agent of God's rule, Jesus has compassion, wills to cleanse the leper, touches the leper, and is able to cleanse him of the leprosy—all reinforced with an immediate effectiveness. At the same time, active faith on the part of the leper is the human posture of trust that gains access to this power—expressed in words and actions. The offering of the sacrifice prescribed by Moses as a testimony to the priests gives public witness (εἰς μαρτύριον) to the cleansing and therefore, indirectly, to the presence of God's rule.

"Secrecy and Openness"

The language about the rule of God is further expressed here by the language of secrecy and openness. Jesus forbids the cleansed leper from saying "anything to anyone" ("Ορα μηδενὶ μηδὲν εἴπῃς), because (by implication from the consequence that occurs when the leper spreads the word) the presence of the crowds would interfere with his efforts to reach the people most needing the rule of God. Nevertheless, the man "proclaimed freely" (κηρύσσειν πολλά) and "spread the word" (διαφημίζειν τὸν λόγον). As a result, such large crowds gathered "that Jesus was no longer able openly to enter into a city" (ὥστε μηκέτι αὐτὸν δύνασθαι φανερῶς εἰς πόλιν εἰσελθεῖν). Jesus then retreated "outside to [otherwise] deserted places" (ἔξω ἐπ' ἐρήμοις τόποις), yet people flocked to him "from everywhere" (πάντοθεν). Clearly "nothing is hidden, except to be made known!" (4:22).

Note the inclusio that frames the episode: "a leper came to him" (1:40) and "people came to him" (1:45). At the beginning, the leper comes alone privately; at the end, despite Jesus' efforts to suppress the report about the cleansing, people come to Jesus even in a desert. The sequence shows how the popularity of Jesus grows. The same progression can also be seen by tracking the references to deserts. The first time Jesus was in a deserted place, he was alone (1:12–13); the second time he is in a deserted place, Peter and those with him tracked him down (1:35–37); and this third time he is in a deserted place, crowds flock to him (1:45).

"The Rule of God"

As we have said, all these word fields—the activity of Jesus, the response of faith, the consequences of support by the crowds and opposition by the authorities—are embedded in the overarching word field of the Gospel, the arrival of the rule of God.

STRUCTURE

This episode is carefully structured so as to set up a situation (a man with leprosy) and resolve it (Jesus cleanses it) and then to present a complication to the resolution (Jesus commands him to silence) that in turn is left unresolved (the former leper spreads the word and makes Jesus' movement difficult) (Noble 278–279). At the same time, this episode is a Markan type-scene of healing. As such, it presents the active presence of the rule of God and the human response of faith that gains access to God's power for healing.

Situation:
    <1:40> And (there) comes to him a leper
Problem:
    begging him
    [and kneeling]

and saying to him,
    "If you want (to),   a
        you are able to cleanse me."   b

Response to the Problem:
    <1:41> And moved by compassion,
        stretching out his hand,
            he touched (him)
    and (he) says to him,
        "I want (to).   a
        Be cleansed."   b

Response:
    <1:42> And immediately the leprosy went from him,   a
    and he was cleansed.   b

Consequence:
    <1:43> And upbraiding him   a
        immediately he drove him out
        <1:44> and (he) says to him,   b
            "See (that) you say nothing to anyone,
    but go show yourself to the priest
    and offer for your cleansing
        what Moses commanded
    as a witness to them.
    <1:45> But going out   a
        he began to proclaim freely   b
    and to spread the word
        with the result that no longer was he able   a
            openly to enter into a city
    but was outside, in deserted places.   b
    and they (people) were coming to him from everywhere.

Note that the patterns of parallelism in the episode clarify how the request of the leper and the response of Jesus with the resulting healing relate to each other. The man requests: (a) "If you want to," (b) "you can cleanse me." Jesus replies: (a) "I do want to," (b) "Be cleansed." Then the narrator recounts: (a) the leprosy left him, and (b) he was cleansed. The parallels demonstrate, first, Jesus' adequate response to the request and then the effective results of Jesus' commands.

There are also parallels in the complications of the action. Jesus (a) drives the man out, and (b) commands the healed leper to say nothing to anyone. Then the narrator tells us that (a) the man went out, but (b) he began to proclaim freely. In an ironic twist, the first words of Jesus (the cleansing) are completely effective, while these second words (the prohibition against spreading the word) are completely controverted. The theological insight to be gained from this is that Jesus has power from God to control demons but no power from God over other humans to control their behavior.

LINGUISTIC COMMENTARY

<1:40> Καὶ ἔρχεται πρὸς αὐτὸν λεπρὸς παρακαλῶν αὐτὸν [καὶ γονυπετῶν] καὶ λέγων αὐτῷ ὅτι Ἐὰν θέλῃς δύνασαί με καθαρίσαι. = **And a leper comes to him begging him [and kneeling] and saying to him, "If you want [to], you are able to cleanse me."**

Καὶ ἔρχεται πρὸς αὐτὸν λεπρὸς

- Καὶ coord. conj. (paratactic/connects this sentence to the previous one, and it introduces a new situation) = **"and"** or **"now."**

- ἔρχεται pres. mid. (in form) ind. 3rd pers. sing. of the verb ἔρχομαι (historical present that introduces a new subject and highlights it) = **"[a leper] comes"** or **"he came."** By putting the verb first (foregrounding), the author stresses the action and at the same time briefly creates suspense regarding the (surprising) subject of the sentence, which comes after the verb and a prepositional phrase = **"Now there comes to him—a leper."** On categorizing the present tense of this verb as a deponent, see comments on Mark 1:7, 9.

- πρὸς αὐτόν prep. phrase with πρός + the accusative, here the acc. sing. masc. of the 3rd pers. personal pronoun αὐτός (object of the preposition) = **"to him"** (Jesus). The prepositional phrase modifies the verb, explaining where the leper is going. Πρός means "to" or "toward" with the implication that the subject ("a leper") reaches his destination.

- λεπρός nom. sing. masc. of the adjective λεπρός, ά, όν (anarthrous substantive use of the adjective as a noun subject) = **"a leprous one"** or **"a leper."** Placing the subject of the sentence last puts emphasis on it. The setting for the leper's appearance is vague.

A leper was impure by virtue of obvious skin lesions or sores or open pustules in which fluids are seeping out of the body. The description here is probably not, however, the modern meaning of the term leper (which refers to someone with Hanson's disease) but nonetheless a potentially serious condition. The impurity probably meant that the leper remained outside the gates of the city and was prohibited from social contact with others. No setting is given here—a narrative omission that may imply Jesus encountered the leper as he was traveling between the "neighboring villages" (1:39). The subsequent command to the leper "to tell no one" reinforces the idea that Mark portrays this episode as a private event on Jesus' travels in which no one else was present.

παρακαλῶν αὐτὸν [καὶ γονυπετῶν] καὶ λέγων αὐτῷ

- παρακαλῶν pres. act. participle nom. sing. masc. of the verb παρακαλέω, agreeing with the subject (λεπρός) of the main clause (a circumstantial participle that, as a present, depicts action contemporaneous with the time of the main verb/ depicts the "manner" by which the leper comes to him) = "**begging**" or "**beseeching**" or "**pleading with**" or "**imploring**" (Williams 42). This is the first in a series of two [or three] participles with a common grammatical identification.

- αὐτὸν acc. sing. masc. of the 3rd pers. personal pronoun αὐτός (direct object of the participle) = "**him**."

- [καὶ coord. conj. (simple connective of two participles) = "**and**."

- γονυπετῶν] pres. act. participle nom. sing. masc. of the verb γονυπετέω (a circumstantial participle that, as a present, depicts action contemporaneous with the time of the main verb/depicts the "manner" by which the leper comes to him) = "**kneeling [down]**" or, literally, "**falling on (his) knees**" (Williams 42). The action reinforces the deference implied by the act of begging. Note the textual uncertainty expressed by the brackets. This variant may not be original in light of Mark's tendency to use a verb that depicts speech (here "pleading") and then immediately after it (without anything else in between) to add the participle λέγων and the words spoken.

- καὶ coord. conj. (simple connective between two participles) = "**and**."

- λέγων pres. act. participle nom. sing. masc. of the verb λέγω (a circumstantial participle of time, which, as a present, depicts action contemporaneous with the time of the main verb)= "**saying**." The "speaking" participle parallels the "begging" participle, because the words that follow the word λέγων convey what the beggar said in begging. As such, what the leper is saying here is not something that occurs in addition to his pleading but rather *is* the precise form that the pleading/saying takes.

Note how the string of present participles convey actions contemporaneous with the action of the main verb. Following a finite verb that is in the historical present, they evoke an experience of immediacy, as if the reader were there experiencing the action all at once. The begging, the falling on his knees, the speaking, and the words that constitute the begging, all these occur simultaneously. The actions together with the words express/embody the leper's faith. In Mark, faith is expressed by action—coming to Jesus, kneeling, and pleading.

- αὐτῷ dat, sing. masc. of the 3rd pers. personal pronoun αὐτός, ἡ, ὅν (indirect object of the participle λέγων) = "**to him (Jesus)**." The quotation that follows is the direct object of the participle λέγων, and the words express what the speaker said.

ὅτι Ἐὰν θέλῃς δύνασαί με καθαρίσαι.

- ὅτι subord. conj. (introduces direct speech, called a recitative ὅτι) to be translated as a comma and quotation marks = ", '. . .'"
- Ἐὰν subord. conj. (introduces a dependent clause, the protasis of a future hypothetical conditional sentence, i.e., a Third Class conditional sentence) = "**if**." Ἐὰν is a combination of εἰ (= "if") + ἄν (a particle expressing uncertainty and signaling a subjunctive to follow). Ἐὰν followed by a subjunctive conveys a hypothetical situation, that is, a situation that may or may not be true now or in the future (Wallace 469–71). As such, the particle limits the force of the verb to specific conditions or circumstances (Smyth 1762). If the condition in the protasis is ever realized, then the conclusion holds true for any time or for all time (Smyth 2337). The entire conditional sentence functions rhetorically as a request.
- θέλῃς pres. act. subj. 2nd person sing. of the verb θέλω (subjunctive in the protasis of a Third Class conditional sentence) θέλω. = "**[if] you are willing**." The present tense of the subjunctive does not convey the time in the present but only an ongoing state in contrast to a single

moment in time (which would be expressed by an aorist subjunctive). The verb θέλω expresses volition and may be translated variously = "**If you want**" or "**If you wish**" or "**If you choose**." Θέλω is a modal or auxiliary verb that requires a complementary infinitive. Here, the complementary infinitive is elided and must be supplied from the explicit complementary infinitive (καθαρίσαι) with the corresponding modal verb δύνασαι in the apodosis that follows. Thus, to render θέλῃς with its elided infinitive, we would translate = "**if you want [to cleanse me]**."

There is an implication to the condition that becomes clear as the story progresses and Jesus touches the man. The leper's uncertain conditional sentence conveys the idea that to heal/cleanse him, Jesus will have to touch him—so is Jesus willing to do this? Thus, the leper challenges Jesus' willingness to heal ("if you will"), without doubting his capacity to do it ("you are able"). Throughout Mark, the verb θέλω is used to express both the human will and the divine will. The challenge of discipleship in Mark is to bring the mind-set (φρονέω) of what humans "want" into line with what God "wants," that is, to be "thinking the things of God rather than to be "thinking the things of humans" (8:33). Note how Jesus prays at Gethsemane, "Not what I want/will, but what you want/will" (14:36). In Mark, it is clearly God's will that people be healed of illnesses.

- δύνασαι pres. mid. (in form) ind. 2nd person sing. of the auxiliary verb δύναμαι (verb in the apodosis of a future hypothetical conditional sentence, which may be in any tense and any mood/auxiliary verb followed by an infinitive) = "**you can**" or "**you are able to**." Wallace (430) lists this verb as a true deponent, but see comments on deponent verbs at Mark 1:4.

In Mark, δύναμαι sometimes, as here, expresses the extent of Jesus' authority—what he "is able" to do (Williams 42). Note also that Mark's word for "miracle" or "work of power" is the cognate noun δύναμις. The verb Δύναμαι can also express the limitations of Jesus' authority. For example, Jesus was "not able (οὐκ ἐδύνατο) to do even one work of power" in his hometown, because of the lack of faith there (6:5–6).

- καθαρίσαι aor. act inf. of the verb καθαρίζω (a complementary infinitive after the auxiliary verb δύνασαι) = "**cleanse**" or "**purify**" (Decker 39; Williams 42). Καθαρίζω is part of the word field of purity/defilement language and here expresses a cleansing from the defilement caused by the "leprosy." The removal of the leprosy will purify the person.

- με acc. sing. masc. or fem. of the first pers. personal pronoun ἐγώ (direct object of the infinitive) = "**me (the leper)**."

<1:41> καὶ σπλαγχνισθεὶς ἐκτείνας τὴν χεῖρα αὐτοῦ ἥψατο καὶ λέγει αὐτῷ, Θέλω, καθαρίσθητι· = **And being moved by compassion, after stretching out his hand, he touched (him), and he says to him, "I want (to). Be cleansed."**

καὶ σπλαγχνισθεὶς ἐκτείνας τὴν χεῖρα αὐτοῦ ἥψατο

- καὶ coord. conj. (paratactic, connects this sentence to the previous sentence) = "**and**."
- σπλαγχνισθείς aor. pass. (in form) participle nom. sing. masc. of the verb σπλαγχνίζομαι, agreeing with the implied subject ("he") of the main verb ἥψατο (a circumstantial participle which, as an aorist, expresses action previous to the time of the main verb) = "**after being filled with compassion**" or "**moved with pity**." The participle may also be causal = "**because he was moved by compassion**" (Decker 39; Williams 42). Some categorize this verb as deponent, but see the critique of this category in the comments on Mark 1:4.

  The noun form of σπλαγχνίζομαι (τὸ σπλάγχνον) refers to the "inner organs" or the "bowels," understood as the physical seat of feelings, in this case, the seat of compassion. It may be contrasted with ὀργίζομαι = to be angry (*EDNT* 2:265). In Mark, the verb is used exclusively of Jesus' compassion. By foregrounding the participle as the first word in the sentence, the author emphasizes that compassion is Jesus' immediate reaction to the leper and that it is the ground for his act of cleansing. For the verb in the variant reading, see Bratcher 66 = "**although Jesus was indignant**" = concessive circumstantial participle.

- ἐκτείνας aor. act. participle nom. sing. masc. of the verb ἐκτείνω (aorist circumstantial participle depicting action previous to the time of the main verb or a participle of attendant circumstance) = "**after stretching out [his hand]**" or "**he put forth [his hand] and**." The root -τεινω with its prefix ἐκ- means to "reach + out" or "stretch + forth." Note that the two participles (σπλαγχνισθείς and ἐκτείνας) run together without a connective, a typical grammatical phenomenon (typical of Mark) known as asyndeton, which in this case shows rapidity of action and closely connects Jesus' compassion with his action.

- τὴν χεῖρα acc. sing. fem. of the noun ἡ χείρ (direct object of the participle ἐκτείνας) = "**the hand**." The article may function here as a possessive pronoun = "**his [Jesus'] hand**." But see below under ἥψατο.
- αὐτοῦ gen. sing. masc. of the 3rd pers. personal pronoun αὐτός, ἡ, -όν (genitive of possession or direct object) = "**his (Jesus') [hand]**" or "**him (the leper)**." This pronoun may function as the direct object of ἥψατο = "**[he touched] him**." See below.
- ἥψατο aor. mid. ind. 3rd pers. sing. of the verb ἅπτω (punctiliar aorist) = "**he touched**." The aorist (depicting completed action), followed by a καί and an historical present (λέγει) may suggest that he touched first and then spoke, in which case the καί is to be understood as a connector of sequential rather than simultaneous actions.

The verb ἥψατο appears to have no direct object (such as "him"), which must be supplied in English. The absence of a direct object gives greater force to the "touching." The narrator may be portraying Jesus' response to the two actions of the leper (pleading and kneeling) with two actions of his own (stretching out and touching).

However, the verb may, in fact, have a direct object. Above, we interpreted the αὐτοῦ that precedes the verb as a personal pronoun that went with τὴν χεῖρα ("his hand"). Now we are suggesting that the αὐτοῦ instead be considered a direct object of ἥψατο, because verbs of sensing such as ἅπτω (in the middle voice) take their direct object in the genitive case. In this case, the article τήν preceding χεῖρα would function as a possessive pronoun and the sentence would be translated = "**Moved by compassion, stretching out the (his) hand, he touched him (the leper)**" (Williams 42). The idea of Jesus' touch is still emphasized, even with a direct object, because the verb is placed last. By placing the verb last, the reader is kept briefly in suspense regarding what Jesus will do.

Jesus touched someone who was unclean. However, instead of being defiled, he cleansed the leper. In Mark's depiction of the rule of God, the dynamics of purity occur in reverse. Instead of the pernicious force of uncleanness defiling Jesus, the holy force of the spirit within Jesus cleanses the leper. Hence, instead of withdrawing from what is unclean, agents of the rule of God invade the realm of uncleanness to bring holiness and wholeness.

In Mark, ἅπτω is an action either of people who touch Jesus in order to be healed or of Jesus when he touches people to heal or bless them. Often, the narrator says that Jesus "lay hands on" people. Here, the use of the word "touch" stresses the extraordinary thing Jesus is doing by making physical contact with an unclean leper.

καὶ λέγει αὐτῷ, Θέλω, καθαρίσθητι·

- καὶ coord. conj. (paratactic, expressing either simultaneous or subsequent speaking in relation to the action of touching) = "**and**" or "**and then**." The context rather than the semantics of καί determines simultaneous or subsequent action. Here, the καί best expresses subsequent action, which allows full weight to be placed on the touching as an action by itself that takes place first before the words are spoken.

- λέγει pres. act. ind. 3rd pers. sing. of the verb λέγω (historical present) = "**he says**" or "**he said**."

- αὐτῷ, dat. sing. masc. of the 3rd pers. personal pronoun αὐτός, ή, όν (indirect object) = "**to him**." The antecedent to the pronoun is "the leper."

- Θέλω, pres. act. ind 1st pers. sing. of the verb θέλω (an intentional present, expressing the state of mind of the speaker) = "**I want (to)**" or "**I am willing**." The intentional present reinforces the intentionality expressed by the root meaning of the verb θέλω. The use of this word provides a parallel to the first part of the leper's request: "I do want [to cleanse you]" is a response to "If you want [to cleanse me]." Again, an elided complementary infinitive (καθαρίσαι) construes with the modal verb θέλω and may be added from the last word spoken by the leper (δύνασαί με καθαρίσαι).

- καθαρίσθητι aor. pass. imperative 2nd pers. sing. of the verb καθαρίζω (pronouncement command) = "**be cleansed**" or "**be made clean**." A pronouncement command is a command that is fulfilled at the moment of speaking by means of the very act of speaking (Wallace 492; Williams 42). The passive voice without an explicit agent being identified may suggest that this is a "divine passive," implying that God is the active agent who does the cleansing. Note that the issue at stake here is not just a healing, but a cleansing, whereby the man can be restored to normal social relationships as well as religious activities at the temple in Jerusalem.

The use of the word καθαρίσθητι echoes the second part of the leper's request: "be cleansed" as a response to the leper's affirmation that "you can cleanse me." Hence, the whole pattern runs like this: Jesus' assertion ("I want to") parallels the protasis of the leper's request ("If you want to"), while Jesus' command ("be cleansed") parallels the apodosis of the leper's request ("you can cleanse me"). The compassion, the reaching out, the touching, and the two words Jesus speaks, all express the immediate and wholehearted response of Jesus to the leper's request.

<1:42> καὶ εὐθὺς ἀπῆλθεν ἀπ' αὐτοῦ ἡ λέπρα, καὶ ἐκαθαρίσθη. = **And immediately the leprosy went away from him and he was cleansed.**

καὶ εὐθὺς ἀπῆλθεν ἀπ' αὐτοῦ ἡ λέπρα

- καί coord. conj. (paratactic, connecting the previous command καθαρίσθητι with the subsequent result ἀπῆλθεν) = "**and.**"

- εὐθύς adverb (temporal, modifies the main verb ἀπῆλθεν and expresses "when" the following event takes place) = "**[and] immediately**" or "**at once**" or "**right away**" or **instantly**" (Decker 42). Here the "immediately" emphasizes the effective authority of Jesus' word of healing.

- ἀπῆλθεν 2nd aor. act. ind. 3rd pers. sing. of the verb ἔρχομαι (punctiliar aorist) = "**[the leprosy] went away**" or "**left**" or "**departed**" or "**disappeared.**" Note how the leprosy is personified and "goes out" of him, functioning similarly to a demon. For categorizing the present tense but not the aorist tense of this verb as deponent, see the comments on Mark 1:7, 9.

- ἀπ' αὐτοῦ prep. phrase with ἀπό + the genitive, here the gen. sing. masc. of the 3rd pers. personal pronoun αὐτός, ἡ, όν (object of the preposition/ genitive of separation) = "**from him.**" The antecedent of the pronoun is "the leper." The prepositional phrase modifies the main verb like an adverb, expressing "where" the leprosy goes. The omicron of ἀπό is elided before a word beginning with a vowel. Note the repetition of ἀπό in the prefix of the verb ἀπῆλθεν and by the preposition ἀπό. The repetition may be captured in translation by using two words = "**away from.**" The repetition emphasizes the completeness of the cleansing of the person from the ailment/defilement.

Jesus and the Leper

- ἡ λέπρα nom. sing. fem. of the noun ἡ λέπρα (subject) = "**the leprosy.**" Note the parallel word order and the contrasting movement between the first sentence of the story ("And there comes to him a leper") and this sentence ("Immediately there went away from him the leprosy"). Putting the subject of the sentence last tends to put emphasis on that word.

καὶ ἐκαθαρίσθη.

- καί coord. conj. (paratactic, connecting this sentence and the previous one) = "**and.**"
- ἐκαθαρίσθη aor. pass. ind. 3rd pers. sing. of the verb καθαρίζω (punctiliar aorist) = "**he was cleansed**" or "**was made clean.**" Note how the two parts of this verse parallel the two words in Jesus' statement. Jesus' words "I want to" parallel "and the leprosy went from him," while Jesus' command "Be cleansed" parallels "and immediately the leprosy went from him." These correlations express an immediate outcome to Jesus' words and thereby emphasize his authority. Jesus reverses the power of impurity to defile. Instead of being defiled by touching the unclean leper, Jesus—anointed with the *holy* spirit—spreads holiness and purifies the leper.

<1:43> καὶ ἐμβριμησάμενος αὐτῷ εὐθὺς ἐξέβαλεν αὐτόν = **And upbraiding him, immediately he drove him out."**

καὶ ἐμβριμησάμενος αὐτῷ

- καί coord. conj. (paratactic) = "**and.**"
- ἐμβριμησάμενος aor. mid. (in form) participle nom. sing. masc. of the deponent verb ἐμβριμάομαι, agreeing with the subject "he" (Jesus) of the verb ἐξέβαλεν (circumstantial participle) = "**upbraiding**" or "**becoming harsh with**" or "**strictly charging**" or "**sternly warning.**" Sometimes this verb is categorized as deponent (Williams 43), but see the critique of this position in the comments on Mark 1:4. While this circumstantial participle is in the aorist, it probably does not express time previous to the time of the main verb, as if it were a separate action from the main verb. Rather it is a description of that in which the main verb consists; that is, the upbraiding *is* what he then does and says. In a sense, then, the participle refers to both verbs that follow

(ἐξέβαλεν and λέγει). The verb implies a stern intent and perhaps anger on Jesus' part, reinforced by the tone of the main verb depicting Jesus as "driving out" the healed leper. The stern intent may be due to Jesus' desire to offset the problems that arise from too much publicity (see below).

If the aorist is to be taken as a separate action that precedes the action of main verb ἐξέβαλεν, then ἐμβριμησάμενος may be translated as "snorting," used of the snorting sound made by horses and depicting the sound a human would make to express great anger or indignation = **"after snorting, he drove him out."** The actions of snorting and driving or casting out characterize exorcisms, and verse 43 may be a remnant of an exorcism that has been incorporated into this healing story. When recounting this story, both Matthew (8:3–4) and Luke (5:13–14) omit any reference to Jesus' snorting and casting out.

- αὐτῷ dat. sing. masc. of the 3rd pers. personal pronoun αὐτός, -ή, -όν (the direct object of ἐμβριμάομαι is in the dative, the case being influenced by the ἐν or ἐμ- in the prefix of the verb) = **"him."** On the other hand, if ἐμβριμησάμενος is translated as "snorting" then the dative case is used here to express the target of the snorting = **"[after snorting] at him."**

εὐθὺς ἐξέβαλεν αὐτόν

- εὐθύς adverb (modifying the finite verb and not the participle, telling *when* Jesus drove him out) = **"immediately."**
- ἐξέβαλεν 2nd aor. act. ind. 3rd person sing. of the verb ἐκβάλλω (punctiliar aorist) = **"he (Jesus) threw out"** or **"he drove out"** or **"drove [him] away"** or **"sent [him] away."** This is a strong word, the same word used to depict the exorcism of demons, although no parallel with demons is implied here since the focus is on Jesus' encounter with this leper.
- αὐτόν acc. sing. masc. of the 3rd pers. personal pronoun αὐτός, ή, όν (direct object) = **"him (the former leper)."**

<1:44> καὶ λέγει αὐτῷ, Ὅρα μηδενὶ μηδὲν εἴπῃς, ἀλλὰ ὕπαγε σεαυτὸν δεῖξον τῷ ἱερεῖ καὶ προσένεγκε περὶ τοῦ καθαρισμοῦ σου ἃ προσέταξεν Μωϋσῆς, εἰς μαρτύριον αὐτοῖς. = **And he says to him, "See that you say nothing**

to anyone (at all) but go show yourself to the priest and offer for your cleansing that which Moses commanded, as a witness to them.

καὶ λέγει αὐτῷ,

- καί coord. conj. (paratactic, connects λέγει with ἐξέβαλεν) = **"and."**
- λέγει pres. act. ind. 3rd pers. sing. of the verb λέγω (historical present) = **"he says"** or **"he said"** or **"he told."**
- αὐτῷ dat. sing. masc. of the 3rd pers. personal pronoun αὐτός, ἡ, ὄν (indirect object) = **"to him."** The speech that follows is the direct object of λέγει. Even though ἐμβριμησάμενος grammatically modifies only ἐξέβαλεν, it is possible that Mark wants us to understand the following words as the words that constitute the "upbraiding."

Ὅρα μηδενὶ μηδὲν εἴπῃς,

- Ὅρα pres. act. impv. 2nd pers. sing. of the verb ὁράω (command in the present tense, thereby expressing a command of continuous action). Here ὅρα has a metaphorical meaning suggesting caution = **"See to it that"** or **"See that"** (Decker 41). Perhaps the imperative stands alone = **"Look!"** as an exclamation to emphasize the command that follows (Williams 43).
- μηδενί dat, sing, masc. of the cardinal number (noun) μηδείς, μηδεμία, μηδέν (indirect object of εἴπῃς) = **"to no one."**
- μηδέν acc. sing. neut. of the cardinal number (noun) μηδείς, μηδεμία, μηδέν (direct object of εἴπῃς) = **"no thing"** or **"not a thing"** or **"nothing."** The double negative in Greek (literally, "nothing to no one") does not equal a positive. Rather, two negatives form an emphatic negative and may be translated **"[say] nothing to anyone at all"** or **"[say] nothing at all to anyone"** (Decker 41; Williams 43).

Note the ironic repetition of this double negative at the end of the Gospel, when the women were commanded to give a message to the disciples, but "they said nothing to anyone at all." When people are reporting a healing, people will report it even when they are commanded not to. However, when the women are to report the resurrection of a man just executed, there is fearful silence.

- εἴπῃς 2nd aor. act. subj. 2nd pers. sing. of the verb λέγω (command) = "say [nothing to anyone]" or "Say nothing—to no one—but go." Although the imperative is not a prohibitive as such, the sentence as a whole functions to prohibit action. Hence, another rendering of the sentence might be = **"Don't tell anyone anything."**

This prohibition is part of the messianic secret motif in Mark. Jesus prohibits the man from telling about his cleansing, partly because Jesus does healings out of compassion and not to gain honor or to gain disciples (he never enjoins anyone he heals to follow him) and partly because he is seeking to head off the hindrances to his activity caused by large crowds, which becomes clear in what follows.

ἀλλὰ ὕπαγε σεαυτὸν δεῖξον τῷ ἱερεῖ

- ἀλλά coord. conj. (adversative, connects ὑπάγει with εἴπῃς) = **"but"** or **"however."** With the two positive commands, one might expect a καί here, which would be translated, "say nothing to anyone and go show yourself to the priest." However, this adversative relates to what the previous clause prohibits. As such, this clause after ἀλλά expresses what the healed man should do instead of speaking to anyone (Decker 41). It expresses a strong contrast.

- ὕπαγε pres. act. impv. 2nd pers. sing. of the verb ὑπάγω (command) = "**go**" or "**go off**." Note the asyndeton, i. e. no καί connective between this imperative and the one to follow, giving the commands a tone of urgency = "**Go show**" or "**Go! Show yourself**." Mark uses ὑπάγω often and exclusively as an imperative. The present imperative is imperfective in that its action is incomplete without the action of the leper showing himself (Decker 41).

- δεῖξον aor. act. impv. 2nd person sing. of the verb δείκνυμι (punctiliar aorist, commanding a single action) = "**show**" or "**present**" (yourself). This aorist imperative and the next one (προσένεγκε) emphasize the specific action commanded by Jesus (Decker 41).

- σεαυτόν acc. sing. masc of the 2nd pers. reflexive pronoun σεαυτοῦ (direct object) = "**yourself**."

- τῷ ἱερεῖ dat. sing. masc. of the noun ὁ ἱερεύς (indirect object) = "**to the priest**." A local priest (who by genealogy was qualified to serve an annual stint in the Temple at Jerusalem) was authorized to examine and declare lepers cleansed or purified, thereby enabling them again to offer sacrifices in the holy place.

καὶ προσένεγκε περὶ τοῦ καθαρισμοῦ σου

- καί coord. conj. (paratactic, connects προσένεγκε with δεῖξον) = "**and.**"
- προσένεγκε 2nd aor. act. impv. 2nd pers. sing. of the verb προσφέρω, (punctiliar aorist, commanding a single action) = "**bring to**" (literally). Because it is used of ritual sacrifices, it should here be translated = "**offer [the sacrifice(s)]**." Considering the plural form of the relative pronoun that follows (see ἅ below), there is probably more than one sacrifice implied here.
- περὶ τοῦ καθαρισμοῦ prep. phrase with περί + the genitive, here with the gen. sing. masc. of the noun καθαρισμός (object of the preposition) = "**for the cleansing**" or "**in exchange for the purification**" or "**in gratitude for the cleansing**" (as a thank-offering for the purification).
- σοῦ gen. sing. masc. (or fem.) of the 2nd pers. personal pronoun σύ (objective genitive; that is, the cleansing of "you"—the implicit direct object of the action of cleansing depicted by the verbal noun καθαρισμοῦ) = "**the cleansing of you**" or "**your purification.**"

Note the repetition in this pericope of the καθαρισ-root, emphasizing not just the healing as such but the purification of the leper. With no modern knowledge of "disease," the concept of illness emphasized the social disjuncture that resulted from the illness. Once cleansed, the leper could now go to the Temple in Jerusalem to offer sacrifices and otherwise resume normal social relationships.

ἃ προσέταξεν Μωϋσῆς, εἰς μαρτύριον αὐτοῖς.

- ἅ acc. plur. neut. of the relative pronoun ὅς, ἥ, ὅ, agreeing in number and gender with its antecedent ("sacrifices"—the implied direct object of προσένεγκε), and it is in the accusative case due to its use in the following dependent clause (as the direct object of προσέταξεν) = "**which**" or "**what.**"
- προσέταξεν aor. act. ind. 3rd pers. sing. προστάσσω (punctiliar aorist)= "**[he] commanded**" or "**ordered**" or he "**prescribed.**"

- Μωϋσῆς nom. sing. masc. of the proper name ὁ Μωϋσῆς (subject of the relative clause) = "**Moses**."

- εἰς μαρτύριον prepositional phrase (expressing purpose or movement toward a goal) with εἰς + the accusative, here acc. sing. neut. of the noun τὸ μαρτύριον (the object of the preposition/the goal of the purpose) = "**for the purpose of [being] a witness**" or "**[serving] as testimony**" (with legal overtones) or "**evidence**" or "**proof**" [that the man was now cleansed].

- αὐτοῖς dat. plur. masc. of the 3rd pers. personal pronoun αὐτός, -ή, -όν (indirect object or a dative of advantage/disadvantage) = "**to them**." There are two syntactical options here. (1) If αὐτοῖς is taken as an indirect object, it belongs syntactically to the verb προσέταξεν = "**which Moses commanded to them as a witness**." This makes little sense and does not account for the placing of αὐτοῖς at the end of the sentence. (2) If αὐτοῖς is not treated as an indirect object, it is either a dative of advantage (in which case the testimony is given "for their benefit") (Decker 42) or a dative of disadvantage (in which case the testimony is given "against them") (Williams 43). A dative of advantage is most likely here, since the sacrifice was, in part, a witness to the authorities and people in general that the certification of the cleansing was complete. Datives are often used in relation to verbal nouns such as μαρτύριον that name the action of their corresponding verbs (cf. the corresponding verb form μαρτυρέω—Smyth 1502; Wallace 173–74) = "**as a testifying for their benefit**" or "**as testimony to them**."

The plural αὐτοῖς is a pronoun whose antecedent is difficult to identify. It refers either to the priests (even though the earlier reference to "the priest" was in the singular) or to the authorities in general or to people in general. If the general prohibition to tell no one is taken seriously, then αὐτοῖς would refer only to the priests, who needed to witness the cleansed state to release the leper back into society. On the other hand, the implication may be that Jesus wants the healing to be revealed by means of the ritual rather than through oral speech.

<1:45> ὁ δὲ ἐξελθὼν ἤρξατο κηρύσσειν πολλὰ καὶ διαφημίζειν τὸν λόγον, ὥστε μηκέτι αὐτὸν δύνασθαι φανερῶς εἰς πόλιν εἰσελθεῖν, ἀλλ' ἔξω ἐπ' ἐρήμοις τόποις ἦν· καὶ ἤρχοντο πρὸς αὐτὸν πάντοθεν. = **But going out he began to proclaim much (freely) and to spread the word, with the result that no**

Jesus and the Leper

longer was he (Jesus) able to enter openly into a city, but he was outside, in deserted places. And people kept coming to him from everywhere.

ὁ δὲ ἐξελθὼν ἤρξατο κηρύσσειν πολλὰ καὶ διαφημίζειν τὸν λόγον,

- ὁ nom. sing. masc. of the definite article ὁ, ἡ, τό (a substantive use of the article, functioning as the subject and serving as a demonstrative pronoun (Smyth 1106; Wallace 211–12; Decker 42; Williams 43) = "**he (the leper)**" or "**that one**" (i.e. the leper).

- δέ postpositive coord. conj. (adversative) = "**but**" or "**however**." Together, ὁ and δέ in Mark signify a change in subject from the subject of the previous sentence, thus making it clear that the leper and not Jesus was the one who went out (Decker 42). The adversative force is strong here, for the man does the exact opposite of what Jesus commands him to do. Jesus has authority over illness to command a cleansing (when the supplicant has faith), but he does not have authority over human will.

- ἐξελθών aor. act. participle nom. sing. masc. of the verb ἐξέρχομαι, agreeing with the subject ὁ (an aorist circumstantial participle expressing time prior to the time of the main verb) = "**after going out**" or "**after he went away**" (Williams 94). This may be a participle of attendant circumstance, which communicates an action coordinate with the action of the main verb (Decker 42; Wallace 279). As such, it would be translated as a finite verb expressing sequential action in parallel with the tense and mood of the main verb = "**but he went out and began**." The verb ἔρχομαι can mean either "to come" or "to go." Here the participle form probably means "going out" or "going away," the movement being signified by the prefix. On the designation of this verb as a deponent in the present tense but not in the aorist, see the comments on Mark 1:7, 9.

- ἤρξατο aor. mid. ind. 3rd person sing of the verb ἄρχω, which, in conjunction with an infinitive, calls attention to the inception or beginning of the action expressed in the infinitive, in this case the action expressed in κηρύσσειν (auxiliary/modal verb used with a complementary infinitive) = "**began**" or "**started**" (Decker 43; Williams 44). In the active voice, ἄρχω means "to rule," but in the middle voice it means "to begin."

- κηρύσσειν pres, act. infinitive of the verb κηρύσσω (complementary infinitive to the auxiliary verb ἄρχομαι, the present tense of the infinitive expressing ongoing action) = "**to proclaim.**" A complementary infinitive functions like the direct object of the auxiliary verb. The infinitive states the action and the auxiliary/modal verb states the particular mode in which that action is being viewed by the speaker. In this case, the auxiliary verb ἤρξατο views the mode of κηρύσσειν as "beginning."

The phrase ἤρξατο κηρύσσειν is a pleonasm (a construction using an auxiliary verb with an infinitive) that could have been expressed by replacing the complementary verb + infinitive with one word, an ingressive imperfect. The choice to use ἤρξατο + an infinitive serves to give emphasis to the actions expressed in the infinitives "to proclaim" and "to spread." The verb ἄρχομαι with a complementary infinitive in the present means to begin to do something and to continue doing that action (Smyth 2128; Wallace 598–99). Thus, the syntax here means to begin and then to continue to proclaim the healing = "**he began to proclaim.**"

- πολλά acc. plur. neut. of the adjective πολύς, (substantive use of the adjective or an adverbial accusative modifying the infinitive in terms of manner or extent) = (as an adjective) "**many things**" or (as an adverb) "**much.**" This typically Markan adverb simply intensifies the verb that it modifies, in this case the infinitive κηρύσσειν, and as such it can be translated by adverbs = "**freely**" or "**extensively**" (Decker 43; Williams 44).

- καί coord. conj. (connective for two infinitives) = "**and.**" The connective could have the implication of result = "and as a result of proclaiming freely to spread the word widely."

- διαφημίζειν pres. act. infinitive of the verb διαφημίζω (a second complementary infinitive to the auxiliary verb ἄρχομαι) = "**to make known**" or "**to spread by word of mouth.**" The prefix διά is an intensifier and suggests that δια-φημίζω should be translated "spread around" or "spread widely" or "disseminate." Again, the present tense signifies ongoing (social) interaction on the part of the leper who had now been cleansed. In particular, the syntax of ἄρχομαι with a present infinitive emphasizes the continuing action of proclaiming by the healed leper—possible now because of his purified state. Because the infinitive has properties not only of a noun but also of a verb, it can take a direct object, here τὸν λόγον.

- τὸν λόγον acc. sing. masc. of the noun ὁ λόγος (direct object of the infinitive διαφημίζειν) = **"the word"** or **"the report [of the healing]."**

In Mark, ὁ λόγος can refer to the message about the rule of God or, more likely here, simply "the word" *about* Jesus or perhaps "the report" of the healing that took place = **"the event"** or **"the matter"** (Decker 43). Obviously, with the combined use of "proclaim" and "the word" to depict the man's actions, the narrator was implying that even a bare report about the healing was indeed spreading the news about the rule of God. In Mark, "word" refers to more than a single word, as, for example, the message of Jesus (cf. 2:2).

ὥστε μηκέτι αὐτὸν δύνασθαι φανερῶς εἰς πόλιν εἰσελθεῖν,

- ὥστε subord. conj. (introducing a result clause) = **"with the result that"** or **"so that."** The conjunction ὥστε introduces a result clause, which usually expresses the main action by means of an infinitive. In Koine Greek, if the subject of the infinitive is the same as the subject of the leading verb, then ὥστε + infinitive denotes anticipated or possible result. If, however, as is the case here, the subject (the leper) of the leading verb (ἤρξατο) is different from the subject (Jesus) of the infinitive δύνασθαι in the ὥστε clause, then ὥστε + infinitive denotes the actual result (Smyth 2257-58; Wallace 592-94). Clearly, as determined both by context and by syntax, the real result of the proclaiming by the leper is being depicted here.

- μηκέτι adverb (modifying the infinitive δύνασθαι) = **"no longer."** Μηκέτι is comprised of a combination of two words, μή (a negative used with verbs and verb forms other than the indicative, here an infinitive) meaning "not" and the adverb ἔτι, which means "still" or "yet." The combination word οὐκέτι rather than μηκέτι is used to negate indicative verb forms. The letter kappa bridges the two words μή and ἔτι. Normally μή would not take a kappa glide consonant before words beginning with a vowel. However, οὐ does take a kappa glide vowel before a smooth breathing, and μηκέτι derives its kappa from analogy with οὐκέτι (Smyth 137b).

- δύνασθαι aor. mid. (in form) infinitive of the deponent verb δύναμαι (infinitive in a result clause) = **"was able."** This infinitive is an auxiliary verb for the infinitive that follows. Wallace (430) lists this verb as a true deponent, but see the comments at Mark 1:4.

- αὐτόν, acc. sing. masc. of the 3rd pers. personal pronoun αὐτός, ή, όν (subject of the infinitive δύνασθαι) = "**he**" (Jesus).

- φανερῶς adverb (manner, modifying the infinitive εἰσελθεῖν) = "**openly**."

- εἰς πόλιν prepositional phrase, expressing motion toward and into, with εἰς + the accusative, here the anarthrous acc. sing. fem. of the noun ἡ πόλις = "**into a city**" or "**town**." The anarthrous noun may suggest that Jesus' reputation was so widespread that he could not enter "*any* city." The prepositional phrase modifies the infinitive εἰσελθεῖν and answers the question "where?"

- εἰσελθεῖν 2nd aor. act. infinitive of the deponent verb ἔρχομαι, (complementary infinitive after the auxilliary/modal verb δύνασθαι, which is also in the form of an infinitive in the aorist, expressing an action occurring without respect to time (Smyth 1967a) = "**to enter**." The repetition of the preposition and the prefix emphasize the entering into.

Some argue that, in Mark's story, Jesus is unable to enter a city openly because he would be prohibited by people from doing so due to his unclean state in having touched a leper. More likely, Mark is portraying Jesus as unable to enter openly into a city because of the huge crowds that would gather as a result of the leper's proclaiming his healing widely. Note how this problem with crowds constrained Jesus to deviate from his plan (expressed in the previous episode) to "go on to the next towns so I might proclaim there too" (1:39). Instead, the healed leper proclaims, despite Jesus' command for him to "tell no one." Jesus cannot control the leper or the crowds and must therefore adapt to this contingency. Perhaps Mark suggests that, as a result, after some days in desert places, Jesus returns to his home in the town of Capernaum (2:1), which he does not have difficulty entering, although crowds quickly gather when they learn of his presence there.

ἀλλ' ἔξω ἐπ' ἐρήμοις τόποις ἦν·

- ἀλλ' coor. conj. (adversative/contrastive) = "**but**" or "**however**." The final alpha of ἀλλά is elided before a word beginning with a vowel. The conjunction contrasts Jesus' inability to enter towns with the resulting necessity to be in deserted places.

- ἔξω adverb (place modifying the verb ἦν) = "**outside**."

- ἐπ' ἐρήμοις τόποις prepositional phrase with ἐπί + the dative, here the anarthrous dat. plur. masc. of the noun ὁ τόπος (object of the preposition/dative of place where) = "**on**" or "**at**" or "**in**" (Decker 44). The final iota of ἐπί is elided before a word beginning with a vowel. The noun τόποις is modified by the adjective ἐρήμοις in the dat. plur. masc. (an adjective modifying τόποις) = "**desert places**" or "**deserted places**."

The phrase portrays places that are isolated and uninhabited, in contrast to the towns (which the narrator has just referenced). These are uninhabited, uncultivated spaces between villages, which would otherwise be deserted. "Outside, in deserted places" is a typical Markan two-step progression in which the first step ("outside") is followed by an emphatic second step ("in deserted places"), which repeats and gives specificity to the first step.

- ἦν impf. act. ind. 3rd person sing. of the verb εἰμί = "**he (Jesus) was**." Note the irony: while previously the leper was consigned outside the cities, now Jesus must be out in deserted places. Εἰμί is not an equative verb here. Rather, it is an intransitive verb that denotes existence = "**he existed**" or "**he stayed**."

καὶ ἤρχοντο πρὸς αὐτὸν πάντοθεν.

- Καί coor. conj. (paratactic, connecting this sentence with the previous one) = "**and**."

- ἤρχοντο impf. mid. (in form) ind. 3rd person plur. of the verb ἔρχομαι (the imperfect of continuous or repeated action) = "**they were coming**" or "**people kept coming**." Note the impersonal plural subject so typical of Markan style. For categorizing the present stem of this verb as deponent, see the comments on Mark 1:7, 9.

- πρὸς αὐτόν prepositional phrase (expressing motion toward) with πρός + the accusative, here the acc. sing. masc. of the 3rd person pronoun αὐτός, -ή, -όν (object of a preposition) = "**to him (Jesus)**."

- πάντοθεν adverb (place, modifying ἤρχοντο). The root πάν- means "all" or "every" and the suffix θεν means "from" = "**from everywhere**" or "**from every quarter**" or "**from all around**." In a previous episode, "everywhere" referred to the "the whole surrounding countryside of Galilee" (1:28).

WHAT FOLLOWS

After several days in deserted places, Jesus returns to his house in Capernaum. Immediately, word about him spreads, and a huge crowd gathers. In the five episodes that follow this episode, Jesus engages in different conflicts resulting from his actions, ordered in a chiastic pattern. Hence, in contrast to the episodes we have just treated where the rule of God has elicited popular support, in the episodes that follow, the rule of God generates conflict, especially with the authorities. As the gospel story unfolds, we learn from every action of Jesus and from every response to it more about the dynamics and values of the rule of God as Mark portrays it.

Conclusion
What Next?

If you have worked through the analyses of the passages in this book, it will help to solidify and expand what you have learned. Here are some suggestions for follow-through.

Identify some basic resources from your own experience and from the bibliography at the end of this book. Which support resources will help you become independent in your work?

Having gone through a complete analysis of passages in this book, evaluate your strengths and weaknesses. Review the grammatical features of nouns and verbs as a basis for making identifications with greater facility. What grammatical features do you know well and which ones do you need to learn? Also, most readers are weak on syntax. So, go over all the syntactical possibilities for each of the cases of nouns, particularly as they occur as objects of prepositions. And do the same for verbs in relation to tenses and moods. You might consider memorizing the options for both nouns and verbs. A review of conjunctions will also serve well.

Consider going back though a passage or a verse that we have covered and then practice the method of analysis until you are able to make the analysis yourself without consulting the book. Read the Greek until you are able to do it with fluidity. Then do the analysis of each word. Weigh the options for semantic meaning and provide a translation of what you have done. Follow the method of analysis until it becomes comfortable to you. Identify the structural dynamics and the patterns of parallelism. The better you know a handful of verses or an entire passage, the easier it will be to tackle new passages.

Choose a passage in Mark not covered here. For example, Mark 3:1–6 would work well. Read the Greek until you do so with ease. Make a tentative translation noting the meanings of words that you do not know. Practice the process of analyzing each word from beginning to end verse by verse. Consult resources where needed. Look for the structure that clarifies the progression of the plot. Discern the patterns of parallelism that illuminate the relationship between parts of the story. Then provide a precise translation that reflects the analysis you have completed. At the end read through the Greek with the understanding you have achieved.

Bibliography

GENERAL USE

Black, David Alan. *Using New Testament Greek in Ministry: A Practical Guide for Students and Pastors*. Grand Rapids: Baker, 1993.
Countryman, L. William. *The New Testament in Greek: A Short Course for Exegetes*. Grand Rapids: Eerdmans, 1993.
Danker, Frederick W. *Multipurpose Tools for Bible Study*. Rev. ed. Minneapolis: Fortress, 1993.
Windham, Neal. *New Testament Greek for Preachers and Teachers: Five Areas of Application*. Lanham, MD: University Press of America, 1991.

GRAMMARS

Adams, A. K. M. *A Grammar of New Testament Greek*. Nashville: Abingdon, 1999.
Blass, F., and A. Debrunner. *A Greek Grammar of the New Testament and Other Early Christian Literature*. Translated and revised by Robert W. Funk. Chicago: University of Chicago Press, 1961.
Brooks, James A., and Carlton L. Winbery. *A Morphology of New Testament Greek: A Review and Reference Grammar*. Lanham: University Press of America, 1994.
Dana, H. E., and Julius R. Mantey. *A Manual Grammar of the Greek New Testament*. New York: Macmillan, 1955.
Moulton, J. H., W. F. Howard, and N. Turner. *Grammar of New Testament Greek*. 4 vols. Edinburgh: T. & T. Clark, 1929–1976.
Mounce, William D. *Basics of New Testament Greek*. Grand Rapids: Zondervan, 1995.
Smyth, Herbert Weir. *Greek Grammar*. Rev. ed. by Gordon M. Messing. Eastford, CT: Martino Fine Books, 2013.

STYLE AND DISCOURSE ANALYSIS

Black, David Alan, ed. *Linguistics and New Testament Interpretation: Essays on Discourse Analysis*. Nashville: B&H Academic, 1992.
Nida, Eugene A., and Johannes P. Louw. *Lexical Semantics of the Greek New Testament*. Resources for Biblical Studies 25. Atlanta: Scholars, 1992.

Nida, E. A., J. P. Louw, and J. Cronje. *Style and Discourse: With Special Reference to the Text of the Greek New Testament*. Cape Town: Bible Society, 1983.
Turner, Nigel. *A Grammar of New Testament Greek*. Vol. 4: *Style*. Edinburgh: T. & T. Clark, 1976.

SYNTAX

Brooks, James A., and Carlton L. Winberry. *Syntax of New Testament Greek*. Lanham, MD: University Press of America, 1979.
Greenlee, J. Harold. *A Concise Exegetical Grammar of New Testament Greek*. 5th ed. Grand Rapids: Eerdmans, 1986.
MacDonald, William G. *Greek Enchiridion: A Concise Handbook of Grammar for Translation and Exegesis*. Peabody, MA: Hendrickson, 1979.
McKay, K. L. *A New Syntax of the Verb in New Testament Greek: An Aspectual Approach*. Studies in Biblical Greek 5. New York: Lang, 1994.
Moule, C. F. D. *An Idiom Book of New Testament Greek*. 2nd ed. New York: Cambridge University Press, 1959.
Nunn, H. P. V. *A Short Syntax of New Testament Greek*. 4th ed. Cambridge: Cambridge University, 1924. Reprint, 1975.
Porter, Stanley E. *Idioms of the Greek New Testament*. Biblical Languages: Greek 2. Sheffield: JSOT Press, 1992.
Smyth, Herbert Weir. *Greek Grammar*. Rev. ed. by Gordon M. Messing. 1920. Reprint, Eastford, CT: Martino Fine Books, 2013.
Wallace, Daniel. *Greek Grammar Beyond the Basics: An Exegetical Syntax of the New Testament with Scripture, Subject, and Greek Word Indexes*. Grand Rapids: Zondervan Academic, 1996.
Zerwick, Max. *Biblical Greek: Illustrated by Examples*. Translated by Joseph Smith. Scripta Pontificii Instituti Biblici 114. Rome: Pontifical Institute, 1963.

READERS GUIDES

Bratcher, Robert G., and Eugene A. Nida. *A Translator's Handbook on the Gospel of Mark*. Helps for Translators 2. London: United Bible Societies, 1961.
Decker, Rodney J. *Mark 1-8: A Handbook on the Greek Text*. Baylor Handbook on the Greek New Testament. Waco: Baylor University Press, 2014.
Friberg, Barbara, and Timothy Friberg. *Analytical Greek New Testament*. Baker's Greek New Testament Library 1. Grand Rapids: Baker, 1981.
Kubo, Sakae. *A Reader's Greek-English Lexicon of the New Testament and A Beginner's Guide for the Translation of New Testament Greek*. Andrews University Monographs 4. Grand Rapids: Zondervan, 1975.
Mason, John, and John Hurtgen. *Reading the New Testament: Exercises for Beginning Readers of the Greek New Testament*. Lewiston, NY: Mellen, 1988.
Williams, Joel F. *Mark*. The Exegetical Guide to the Greek New Testament. Nashville: B&H Academic, 2020.

BIBLIOGRAPHY

TEXTUAL COMMENTARY

Metzger, Bruce. *A Textual Commentary on the Greek New Testament: A Companion Volume to the United Bible Societies' Greek New Testament (Fourth rev. ed.).* 2nd ed. Stuttgart: Deutsche Bibelgesellschaft, 1994.

Omanson, Roger L. *A Textual Guide to the Greek New Testament: An Adaptation of Bruce Metzger's Textual Commentary for the Needs of Translators.* Stuttgart: Deutsche Bibelgesellschaft, 2006.

GRAMMATICAL/TRANSLATION AIDS

Reinecker, Fritz, and Cleon Rogers. *Linguistic Key to the Greek New Testament.* Grand Rapids: Zondervan, 1976.

Zerwick, Max, and Mary Grosvenor. *A Grammatical Analysis of the Greek New Testament.* 5th ed. Rome: Pontifical Biblical Institute Press, 1996.

FEATURES OF GREEK: SPECIALIZED STUDIES

Carson, D. A. *A Student's Manual of New Testament Greek Accents.* Grand Rapids: Baker, 1985.

Fanning, Buist M. *Verbal Aspect in New Testament Greek.* Oxford Theological Monographs. Oxford: Clarendon, 1990.

Noble, David. "An Examination of the Structure of St. Mark's Gospel." PhD diss., University of Edinburgh, 1972.

Pennington, Jonathan T. "Deponency in Koine Greek: the Grammatical Question and the Lexicographical Dilemma." *Trinity Journal* 24 (2003) 55–76.

———. "Setting Aside 'Deponency': Rediscovering the Greek Middle Voice in New Testament Studies." In *The Linguist as Pedagogue: Trends in the Teaching and Linguistic Analysis of the Greek New Testament,* edited by Stanley E. Porter and Matthew Brook O'Donnel, 181–203. New Testament Monographs 11. Sheffield: Sheffield Phoenix, 2009.

Porter, Stanley E. *Verbal Aspect in the Greek of the New Testament, With Reference to Tense and Mood.* Studies in Biblical Greek 1. New York: Lang, 1989.

Taylor, Bernard A. "Deponency and Greek Lexicography." In *Biblical Greek Language and Lexicography: Essays in Honor of Frederick W. Danker,* edited by Bernard A. Taylor et al., 167–76. Grand Rapids: Eerdmans, 2004.

Thrall, Margaret. *Greek Particles in the New Testament: Linguistic and Exegetical Studies.* New Testament Tools and Studies 3. Grand Rapids: Eerdmans, 1962.

DICTIONARIES

The Analytical Greek Lexicon. Grand Rapids: Zondervan, 1969.

Balz, Horst, and Gerhard Schneider, eds. *Exegetical Dictionary of the New Testament.* 3 vols. Grand Rapids: Eerdmans, 1990–1993. (*EDNT*)

BIBLIOGRAPHY

Bromiley, Geoffrey W., ed. *Theological Dictionary of the New Testament*. 1 vol. abridgement of Kittel. Grand Rapids: Eerdmans, 1985.
Danker, Frederick W. *A Greek-English Lexicon of the New Testament and Other Early Christian Literature*. 3rd ed. Chicago: University of Chicago Press. (BDAG)
Kittel, Gerhard, and Gerhard Friedrich, eds. *Theological Dictionary of the New Testament*. 10 vols. Translated by Geoffrey W. Bromiley. Grand Rapids: Eerdmans, 1964-76.
Liddell, H. G., and R. A. Scott. *An Intermediate Greek-English Lexicon*. Oxford: Clarendon, 1889.
Louw, J. P., and E. A. Nida *A Greek-English Lexicon of the New Testament Based on Semantic Domains*. 2 vols. 2nd ed. New York: United Bible Societies, 1989.
Spicq, Ceslas. *Theological Lexicon of the New Testament*. 3 vols. Translated by James Ernest. Peabody, MA: Hendrickson, 1994.

VOCABULARY AIDS

Black, David Alan. *Linguistics for Students of New Testament Greek: A Survey of Basic Concepts and Applications*. Grand Rapids: Baker, 1988.
Brooks, James A., and Carlton L. Winbery. *A Morphology of New Testament Greek: A Review and Reference Grammar*. Lanham, MD: University Press of America, 1994.
Robinson, Thomas A. *Mastering Greek Vocabulary*. 2nd ed. Peabody, MA: Hendrickson, 1990.
Rogers, Thomas. *Greek Word Roots: A Practical List with Greek and English Derivatives*. Grand Rapids: Baker, 1981.
Scott, Bernard Brandon. *Reading New Testament Greek: Complete Word Lists and Reader's Guide*. Peabody, MA: Hendrickson, 1993.
Stehle, Matthias. *Greek Word Building*. Rev. by Herbert Zimmerman. Translated by F. Forrester Church and John S. Hanson. Sources for Biblical Study 10. Missoula, MT: Scholars, 1976.
Trenchard, Warren C. *Complete Vocabulary Guide of the Greek New Testament: Complete Frequency Lists, Cognate Groups & Principal Parts*. Rev. ed. Grand Rapids: Zondervan, 1998.
Van Voorst, Robert E. *Building Your New Testament Greek Vocabulary*. 3rd ed. Resources for Biblical Study 43. Atlanta: Society of Biblical Literature, 2001.

INTERLINEARS

Marshall, Alfred. *The Interlinear Greek-English New Testament: The Nestle Greek Text with a Literal English Translation*. Grand Rapids: Zondervan, 1958.

CONCORDANCES

Bachmann, H., and Wolfgang A. Slaby, eds. *Computer-Konkordanz zum Novum Testamentum Graece von Nestle-Aland, 26. Auflage, and zum Greek New Testament, 3rd edition*. New York: de Gruyter, 1980.

BIBLIOGRAPHY

Moulton, W. F. and A. S. Geden. *A Concordance to the Greek Testament*. 5th ed. rev. by H. K. Moulton. Edinburgh: T. & T. Clark, 1897.

Wigram, George V. *An Englishman's Greek Concordance of the New Testament*. Peabody, MA: Hendrickson, 1994.

www.ingramcontent.com/pod-product-compliance
Lightning Source LLC
Chambersburg PA
CBHW030113170426
43198CB00009B/608